THE INVESTOR'S
GUIDEBOOK TO

ALTERNATIVE
INVESTMENTS

THE INVESTOR'S GUIDEBOOK TO

ALTERNATIVE INVESTMENTS

The Role of Alternative Investments in Portfolio Design

STUART R. VEALE

Prentice Hall Press

PRENTICE HALL PRESS
Published by the Penguin Group
Penguin Group (USA) LLC
375 Hudson Street, New York, New York 10014

USA | Canada | UK | Ireland | Australia | New Zealand | India | South Africa | China

penguin.com

A Penguin Random House Company

Library of Congress Cataloging-in-Publication Data

Veale, Stuart R.
The investor's guidebook to alternative investments : the role of alternative investments
in portfolio design / Stuart R. Veale.— First edition.
            p.   cm
            Includes index.
        ISBN 978-0-7352-0530-7 (pbk.)
    1. Investments.   2. Portfolio management.   I. Title.
            HG4521.V43   2013
        332.6—dc23   2013024183

First edition: October 2013

PRINTED IN THE UNITED STATES OF AMERICA

10 9 8 7 6 5 4 3 2 1

PUBLISHER'S NOTE: This publication is designed to provide accurate and authoritative
information in regard to the subject matter covered. It is sold with the understanding that
the publisher is not engaged in rendering legal, accounting, or other professional services.
If you require legal advice or other expert assistance, you should seek the services
of a competent professional. Continued on page 218.

While the author has made every effort to provide accurate telephone numbers,
Internet addresses, and other contact information at the time of publication, neither the publisher
nor the author assumes any responsibility for errors, or for changes that occur after publication.
Further, the publisher does not have any control over and does not assume any
responsibility for author or third-party websites or their content.

Most Prentice Hall Press books are available at special quantity discounts for bulk purchases for sales
promotions, premiums, fund-raising, or educational use. Special books, or book excerpts, can
also be created to fit specific needs. For details, write: Special.Markets@us.penguingroup.com.

This book is dedicated to:

*the ever-increasing number of investors who are perceptive enough
to realize that the Western nations are collectively heading down
the wrong path and have the courage to take the actions necessary
to protect themselves and their families.*

FREE NEWSLETTER

The field of alternative investments is changing constantly. To keep updated on changes, simply send your email address to stu@invest-perform.com. In exchange, you'll receive a complimentary copy of Alternative Investment Quarterly Newsletter. I also welcome your comments, critiques, and ideas.

This book was developed using sources believed to be reliable but which are not guaranteed. Opinions, estimates, and forecasts constitute the author's judgment as of the date this material was submitted and is subject to change without notice. Past performance is not indicative of future results. This material is not intended as an offer or solicitation for the purchase or sale of any instrument. Securities, financial instruments, or strategies mentioned herein may not be suitable for all investors. The opinions and recommendations herein do not take into account individual client circumstances, objectives, or needs and are not intended as recommendations of particular securities, financial instruments, or strategies to particular clients. Each reader must make independent decisions regarding any securities or financial instruments mentioned herein.

CONTENTS

FOREWORD

I finished the second edition of my book on investing called *Stocks, Bonds, Options, Futures (SBOF)* in 2001. Here we are 12 years later. While the second edition was still selling well, it was also overdue for an update. Over the last 12 years, much has changed in the way stocks and bonds were priced, traded, analyzed, packaged, and marketed. Specialists on the New York Stock Exchange were replaced with designated market makers. The volume of trades executed on the dark pools soared. Derivatives on rainfall and wind had become hot products. Twenty-four-hour trading became a reality. The variety of exotic options exploded. Exchange traded funds became the fastest-growing financial product in history, etc.

While I started out to write the third edition of *SBOF*, it quickly became clear the industry had become too broad and too complex to comfortably fit in one text. Therefore, after discussing it with my publisher and readers, I made the decision to break the book into four manageable volumes:

- *The Investor's Guidebook to Derivatives*
- *The Investor's Guidebook to Alternative Investments*
- *The Investor's Guidebook to Fixed Income Investments*
- *The Investor's Guidebook to Equities*

My hope is that by expanding the book into four volumes, I'll be able to make them more comprehensive, include more examples, and make the books more useful to my readers. While I made every effort to proof the text, there will undoubtedly be errors for which I assume full responsibility. It is my intent to update these volumes frequently and therefore I welcome my readers' suggestions on which topics should be added, expanded, and omitted in future editions. Please email your questions, critiques, and comments to stu@invest-perform.com. I hope to answer every email I receive.

This book was prepared from sources believed to be reliable but which are not guaranteed. The research analyst(s) who is primarily responsible for this research and whose name is listed on the front cover certifies that: (1) all of the views expressed in this research accurately reflect his or her personal views about any and all of the subject securities or issuers; and (2) no part of any of the research analyst's compensation was, is, or will be directly or indirectly related to the specific recommendations or views expressed by the research analyst in this research. Opinions and estimates constitute our judgment as of the date of this material and are subject to change without notice. Past performance is not indicative of future results. This material is not intended as an offer or solicitation for the purchase or sale of any financial instrument. Securities, financial instruments, or strategies mentioned herein may not be suitable for all investors. The opinions and recommendations herein do not take into account individual client circumstances, objectives, or needs and are not intended as recommendations of particular securities, financial instruments, or strategies to particular clients. The recipient of this report must make its own independent decisions regarding any securities or financial instruments mentioned herein.

PREFACE

The first step in studying alternative investments is to define them. Unlike equities and debt, which have very specific definitions, reasonable investors disagree over what constitutes an "alternative investment." For example, some investors would certainly define the following as alternative investments:

- Private equity programs
- Equity option overwrite program
- Long/short equity programs
- Takeover arbitrage programs
- Convertible bond arbitrage strategies
- Mezzanine debt strategies

Their justification for considering these investments to be alternative investments is that they behave somewhat differently from simply going long or short on a portfolio of equities or debt. That may be true, but decisions to be primarily long or short equities, write or not write options against existing positions, or overweight stocks that you believe are takeover candidates are better described as tactical equity strategies than as alternative investments. In this book, strategies that incorporate traditional stocks and bonds are not considered alternative investments, but instead are substrategies within their respective asset classes. Examples of alternative investments discussed in this book include investments in:

- Precious metals
- Gemstones
- Energy exploration partnerships
- REITs and real estate partnerships
- Collectibles (numismatic coins, artwork, stamps, cars, rare watches, vintage jewelry, rare furniture)

Today's smart investors allocate a higher percentage of their investments to alternative investments and have expanded the universe of alternative investments they are considering for their portfolios. This book explains why. The first half of the book discusses the rationale for overweighting alternative investments in today's portfolios. Some will say that the first part of this book has a "conservative" political perspective because most conservatives draw the same conclusions from the information presented. However, numbers don't lie and the laws of economics are, in their own way, as irrefutable and inevitable as the laws of physics. Thus, instead of conservative I would prefer to describe this book's perspective as realistic and pragmatic. To the extent that being realistic and pragmatic is also regarded as being conservative—so be it. At the seminars I give on alternative investments, the vast majority of attendees describe themselves as conservative.

After the first part of the book makes the case for alternative investments, the second part of this book provides in-depth overviews of the major types of alternative investments. For those interested in the mathematics of calculating the projected risk and reward of a multi-asset class portfolio, the appendix provides both an explanation of the calculations as well as example calculations.

CHAPTER ONE

Why Alternative Investments?

There are numerous reasons why alternative investments are currently drawing such high levels of interest from investors. While it is hard to rank the reasons in order of significance—and the order would undoubtedly be different for different investors—the most important one is that around the world, people are losing faith in the ability of sovereign governments and the world's largest banks to remain solvent. Unfortunately, this lack of faith in our most important institutions isn't affecting just one country. It is impacting over half of the world's population. It starts with the United States, and includes half of Europe, Japan, parts of Latin America, parts of South America, most of the Middle East, and parts of Africa.

For better or worse, politics and investing are inextricably intertwined. When the political and economic future looks bright, traditional stocks and bonds tend to outperform alternative investments. However, when the future is (at best) uncertain, alternative investments often offer investors a better reward/risk trade-off. So, while this book covers the alternative investments, it also looks in some depth at historical and current political environments and their impact on the return of alternative investments. It is impossible to understand why alternative investments perform better during periods of economic and political uncertainty without putting the relationship between them into an historical context.

Most civilizations/countries that have failed were not conquered from outside their borders—at least not initially. Instead, most of the civilizations/countries that collapsed have done so from within, as a result of gross mismanagement. It doesn't matter if the government is headed by a king/queen, general or colonel, prime minister, president, parliament, proconsul, dictator, central committee, assembly, congress, village elders, or the village idiot—the pattern of behavior on the part of the government from the birth of the new thriving civilization until the collapse of that same civilization is remarkably consistent.

Starting a new civilization often requires that the initial citizens overcome huge barriers and make great sacrifices. As a result, when a new civilization is born its new government usually starts by respecting those sacrifices and acting responsibly. The initial leaders put the country's interests ahead of their own interests and the country's long-term interests ahead of any short-term political considerations. They do this by:

- Balancing their annual budgets
- Establishing and maintaining financial reserves
- Doing strategic long-term planning
- Making necessary, well-designed, and fully funded investments in infrastructure
- Providing proper maintenance for their assets
- Managing their natural resources responsibly
- Ensuring that all transactions between the government and its vendors are fully vetted, transparent, and conducted at arm's length

- Funding all the future liabilities it incurs on a current basis
- Eliminating political corruption
- Maintaining a fair and independent judiciary
- Doing the right thing—even if it costs the leaders their jobs, perks, or offices

However, sooner or later—often sooner—every government throughout history wanted to spend more than it could collect in taxes. Whether to indulge a lavish lifestyle fit for a king, or to fund a war or series of wars against neighbors or domestic political opponents, or simply to "buy" the loyalty of the voters who want to receive more in services than they are willing to pay in taxes, the slippery slope from a "responsible well-managed government" to a "self-serving government" follows a familiar and often repeated downward spiral. Instead of funding construction projects out of taxes, the government starts borrowing money "on the books"—but justifies the borrowing by only using it to fund "capital projects" such as bridges, roadways, and the like. The argument is that the new bridge will last 50 years or more, so it is OK to pay for them over the long term. These projects are viewed as investments—not consumption, and that distinction makes it OK to borrow money to fund them. You may or may not agree.

Next, the government fails to adequately fund its future liabilities like government employee pension and promised health-care benefits—kicking the can down the road to future taxpayers. Over the short term this keeps government employees, taxpayers, and politicians happy because:

- Government employees believe they will receive the benefits promised by the government.
- Taxpayers receive the services of the government employees, yet their taxes stay low—at least for the time being.

- Politicians, by promising benefits to the employees but not raising the taxes required to pay for them, get reelected by both groups!

Since both government employees and taxpayers get what they want over the short term, neither side pays much attention to the budget details. Typically, the generation that will get stuck with the bill is just being born and not yet of voting age when the funding gap starts to grow.

The government then starts to borrow money "on the books" to meet its basic operating expenses—the financial equivalent of putting this month's rent on a charge card. This is easier politically than cutting spending or raising taxes. While some informed, concerned, and responsible citizens will object, most are too disinterested or lack the education to understand and fully appreciate the future ramifications of an ever increasing debt load. Once borrowing to pay operating expenses starts, it becomes politically addictive and the principal balance grows exponentially over time to a size that's so large (to a multiple of the country's GDP) that it becomes impossible to repay the debt—at least not without severely depreciating the country's currency.

Government spending increases as a percent of GDP. As it does, politicians gain more power over the economy. As the government gains more power over the economy, instead of pure market forces allocating capital efficiently, capital allocation becomes increasingly tied to "pay to play policies" and "crony capitalism." The government steers the lion's share of the government contracts and other economic opportunities to its campaign contributors and other supporters. Politicians can also pass rules and regulations that punish foes and reward supporters. Some companies and individuals feel forced to contribute to all parties, just to make sure they aren't locked out of the government spending process or discriminated against by government bureaucrats.

Having nearly exhausted its ability to borrow on its books, the government then shifts some of its borrowing to "off balance sheet financing" to hide the true extent of its debt. It does so by creating and having agencies issue their own debt—or by doing certain types of "interest rates" and "FX swaps" that are really just loans in disguise.

With cash becoming tight, the government delays or simply omits necessary maintenance and upgrades on roads, bridges, power grids, air-traffic control systems, airports, port facilities, and, as a result, they slowly corrode and become unsafe and/or break down. Becoming increasingly desperate for cash, the government raids any trust funds that are available and replaces them with IOUs and/or secretly borrows against the country's gold reserves, energy resources, water resources, and other assets.

Finally, all other options being exhausted, the government simply debases its money by making its coins smaller, diluting the precious metal content of its coins, or by simply printing excessive amounts of paper money to service its debts. While the buying power of the currency plunges, the country's politicians can pretend that the country is honoring its commitments. If the government also controls the procedures used to calculate inflation, unemployment, and the money supply, it can manipulate them in an attempt to hide the truth from its citizens.

As the population loses faith in the currency, the government imposes currency controls, manufactures "pretenses" to seize private assets, jails its opposition, and imposes other desperate and ultimately self-defeating strategies. These last steps always lead to a complete collapse of the currency and the economy.

This sad progression has been repeated hundreds of times

throughout history. Once a country starts down this slippery slope, the progression tends to accelerate, as shown in Figure 1.1. Naturally, the progression is not purely sequential. Elements overlap in time and don't necessarily occur in the order just described.

FIGURE 1.1

Typical Country Financial Death Spiral

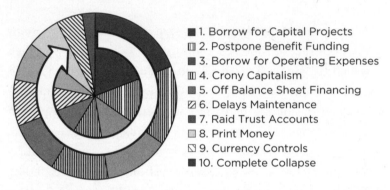

■ 1. Borrow for Capital Projects
▥ 2. Postpone Benefit Funding
■ 3. Borrow for Operating Expenses
▥ 4. Crony Capitalism
■ 5. Off Balance Sheet Financing
▨ 6. Delays Maintenance
■ 7. Raid Trust Accounts
□ 8. Print Money
◩ 9. Currency Controls
■ 10. Complete Collapse

In addition to the financial death spiral, there are other reasons why investors are increasing their allocations to alternative investments, such as:

- The United States has set a standard of living that is envied around the world.
- The current low returns of traditional investments—particularly bonds—is a real problem for retirees, insurance companies, pension plans, and anyone else who's trying to earn a safe positive return on capital.
- The traditional markets have become "more efficient"—making it harder to outperform.
- Investors have less faith that corporate management will place their interests first.

- Tax rates on traditional investments are rising so the tax advantages offered by some alternative investments are becoming more valuable on a relative basis.
- The variety of alternative investments keeps increasing—providing investors with additional choices enabling them to find ones in which they are comfortable investing and/or have some expertise.
- The investor enjoys a hobby (numismatic coins, restoring antique cars, restoring old furniture) and wants to turn their hobby into a profitable venture.
- The investor expects the alternative investment to have a low correlation with traditional stocks and bonds and therefore improve the return/risk portfolios when they are added to traditional portfolios.

Some of these are self-explanatory. Others deserve additional discussion—starting with the envy of the US standard of living. Throughout Asia, Africa, Eastern Europe, and the Middle East, people aspire to obtaining a US standard of living. Even the so-called poor in the United States lead lives that are the envy of many of the world's inhabitants with TVs, electricity, clean running water and indoor plumbing, access to free education, access to free health care, access to food, and so on. Unfortunately, there simply isn't enough iron or copper or zinc in the ground to allow the billions of humans on the earth to enjoy a US standard of living. For example, a typical US house and car includes 440 and 65 pounds of copper, respectively. There is not enough copper in the ground for everyone to have a house and car that contains this much copper. As other nations try to catch up to the United States, the law of supply and demand will force the real cost of all metals and minerals higher.

As of this writing, the 10-year treasury is yielding approximately 1.75%. Even using the US government's terribly flawed measure, inflation exceeds 2%. Thus, investors seeking a real positive return have to look elsewhere. With the real rate of inflation around 6% (source: Shadowstats.com) investors are effectively being taxed at a 343%+ tax rate (6%/1.75%) on investment income. There's nothing like a negative real return on traditional investment to cause investors to seek out alternatives.

As the number of investors and analysts looking at traditional investments increases, the probability of outperforming decreases. Said another way, what are the odds that you are going to learn something significant about IBM common stock that the hundreds of analysts and millions of investors who have already examined it have overlooked? However, for some alternative investments, each example is unique, such as:

- A rare coin can either be worth "tens of thousands" or "hundreds of thousands" of dollars depending upon very subtle differences in wear. A keen eye, or luck at a garage or estate sale, can make a huge difference.
- Each gemstone is unique. Most gemstones trade privately instead of at public auctions. Middlemen buy stones from miners, have them cut and polished, and offer the stones to a few investors. Thus, with gemstones, who you know is as important as what you know about the stones.
- A site to drill an oil well can be very under or overpriced—depending upon whether oil is found there. Geological skill and experience at reading subterranean structures can provide a very meaningful advantage.

Paralleling the decline in faith in government and banks, investors have lost faith in corporate management after Enron,

WorldCom, Conseco, HealthSouth, Washington Mutual, Parmalat, Lehman Brothers, Bear Stearns, General Motors, CIT, Chrysler, MF Global, Thornburg Mortgage, Ascot (Madoff), Countrywide, etc. Many investors are convinced that too many management teams are either incompetent, unethical, or just plain greedy. They would rather trust their investments to physical "stuff" and eliminate the ethics risk.

The bottom line is that there is no shortage of reasons why investors are becoming increasingly interested in alternative investments. (A discussion of how to quantify the benefit of adding alternative assets to the return and risk of a portfolio is presented in the appendix.) Let's start by looking at the world's most commonly owned alternative investment—gold.

CHAPTER TWO

Introduction to Gold

The most common alternative asset class is gold. Almost everyone owns some—even if it is just a gold-plate ring or a pair of tiny gold earrings. Before we look at gold as an investment, let's review some of gold's characteristics.

BASIC GOLD FACTS

- Gold is element number 79, symbol Au. As an element, it can't be subdivided any further without being broken into subatomic particles.
- Gold is a noble metal, meaning that it doesn't rust or corrode. Take a shiny ounce of gold. Throw it into the ocean. Come back in 1,000 years. Find the coin. You still have a shiny 1-ounce gold coin. Gold is virtually indestructible.
- Gold is highly conductive yet doesn't tarnish. For this reason, it is used in circuits and to coat the connective ends of cables.

- Gold is very unreactive, which is why it is found as flakes or nuggets of nearly pure gold and why gold is used to coat biological implants.
- Gold easily creates alloys, especially with silver, platinum, and palladium.
- Gold is heavy. A 15-inch cube would weigh about 1 ton.
- Gold is malleable. One ounce of gold can be beaten into a 100-square-foot sheet or drawn into a wire 60 miles long. The wire can be 1/400th as thick as a human hair. Pure 24-karat gold is soft enough to be molded with hand pressure.
- Gold is rare. The total amount of aboveground gold found from 10,000 BC until now is between 150,000 and 175,000 metric tons—that makes a 75- to 90-foot cube (one-third of the Washington Monument). The reason the amount can't be estimated with more accuracy is that families often pass gold from generation to generation.
- Gold is not too rare. There is enough so that everyone on the planet could have between 1 and 2 ounces—if the world's gold was equally divided among humanity.
- Gold has been the ultimate brand name for 10,000 years. In the New Testament of the Bible, the Wise Men brought gold—not T-bills. High-end charge cards are known as "gold cards." The highest standard is the "gold standard."
- Gold has universal global appeal. Walk into any room in any country in the world and ask, "Who would like some gold?" The answer is always "everyone."
- Gold is made available in different purities. Because gold is so soft, it is frequently mixed with other metals to strengthen it. Most gold is stamped with a purity value, as shown in Figure 2.1. Pure gold is 24 karats (K).

FIGURE 2.1

Karat Value vs. Purity

Karat	Purity
8K	.333
10K	.416
14K	.583
16K	.666
18K	.750
22K	.916
24K	1.000

- Gold is measured in at least five different units of weight: troy ounces (t oz), avoirdupois ounces (oz), grams (g), pennyweights (DWT), and carats. Figure 2.2 shows the relationship of the various units to each other.

FIGURE 2.2

Weight Conversions Used for Gold

1 ounce troy	= 31.1033 grams		1 gram	= 5.0 carats
1 ounce troy	= 20 DWT		1 gram	= .643 DWT
12 ounces troy	= 1 pound troy		1.5552 grams	= 1.00 DWT
14.5833 ounces troy	= 1 pound avoirdupois		28.3405 grams	= 1 ounce avoirdupois
0.9114 ounce troy	= 1 ounce avoirdupois		240 DWT	= 1 pound troy
32.15 ounce troy	= 1 kilogram		643.21 DWT	= 1 kilogram
1 kilogram	= 2.68 pounds troy		18,2291 DWT	= 1 ounce avoirdupois
1 kilogram	= 35.2740 ounces avoirdupois		1 kilogram	= 2.2046 pounds avoirdupois

- Gold is smelted in three colors:
  - Yellow gold is either pure 24K gold or 14K to 22K gold mixed with copper and zinc.

- Rose gold is gold mixed with copper. (Rose gold can be 22K to 18K.)
- White gold is gold mixed with platinum and often coated with rhodium for added shine and hardness.

Gold has been used as an investment to store wealth and as a currency. Let's first look at gold's historic role as money.

CHAPTER THREE

A Concise History of Gold as Money

In order to appreciate gold's usefulness as an alternative invest-ment it is essential to understand gold's historic roles both as a store of wealth and as a currency.

Aristotle defined the five essential characteristics of money:

- **Durable**—As we mentioned earlier, gold is virtually inde-structible.
- **Divisible**—Gold can be reduced into very small units. In some countries, cards with a single embedded gram of gold are commonly used as currency.
- **Consistent**—The aboveground supply of gold is equal to 100 times the annual production, so the supply of gold is remark-ably consistent. The supply increases at about the same rate as the population. No government can just "print it."
- **Portable**—Oil has many of the same characteristics as gold, but oil is much harder to move, store, and subdivide. Gold is very convenient because it is compact and portable.
- **Has value in and of itself**—Unlike paper with green ink,

gold is useful in its own right as jewelry, in medicine, in electronics, and so forth. Its value has never been zero. Since you can hold gold in your hand unencumbered, it is not an asset that's someone else's liability—unlike a CD, bond, or mortgage.

Gold also helped define the two roles that money plays:

- First, it allows goods to sell as one price. Before the creation of "money," goods had to be traded by barter. If you had a wagon of wheat to sell, you had to think about how many chickens you would take for your wheat, how many goats, how many blankets, how many barrels of ale, etc. After the creation of money, your wheat would only have "one price" expressed in gold, as would the other goods, making it much easier for commerce to occur.
- Second, it allows the storage of wealth. Once again, think about that wagon of wheat. After you sell your wheat and buy what you need, if you still have gold left over, you can take it home and "store your wealth." While the wheat can't be stored indefinitely, gold can. Gold can then take care of you if you become ill, injured, too old to work, or simply no longer want to work.

Throughout history, gold competed against all of the other elements and has been repeatedly selected by successive civilizations to be used as money. No one person designated that gold be used, no government issued an edict that gold would be used as money. Gold simply competed against all of the other elements and won!

If you look at all the elements in the periodic table (Figure 3.1), most can't be used as money because they are:

- Too common—like carbon
- Too rare—like berkelium
- Radioactive—like radon
- Reactive—like sodium
- Gaseous—like argon

FIGURE 3.1

The Periodic Table

Group→	1	2	3	4	5	6	7	8	9	10	11	12	13	14	15	16	17	18
Period 1	1 H																	2 He
2	3 Li	4 Be											5 B	6 C	7 N	8 O	9 F	10 Ne
3	11 Ne	12 Mg											13 Al	14 Si	15 P	16 S	17 Cl	18 At
4	19 K	20 Ca	21 Sc	22 Ti	23 V	24 Cr	25 Mn	26 Fe	27 Co	28 Ni	29 Cu	30 Zn	31 Ga	32 Ge	33 As	34 Se	35 Br	36 Kr
5	37 Rb	38 Sr	39 Y	40 Zr	41 Nb	42 Mo	43 Tc	44 Ru	45 Rh	46 Pd	47 Ag	48 Cd	49 In	50 Sn	51 Sb	52 Te	53 I	54 Xe
6	55 Cs	56 Ba		72 Hf	73 Ta	74 W	75 Re	76 Os	77 Ir	78 Pt	79 Au	80 Hg	81 Tl	82 Pb	83 Bi	84 Po	85 At	86 Rn
7	87 Fr	88 Ra		104 Rf	105 Db	106 Sg	107 Bh	108 Hs	109 Mt	110 Ds	111 Rg	112 Cn	113 Uut	114 Fl	115 Uup	116 Lv	117 Uus	118 Uuo

Lanthanides	57 La	58 Ce	59 Pr	60 Nd	61 Pm	62 Sm	63 Eu	64 Gd	65 Tb	66 Dy	67 Ho	68 Er	69 Tm	70 Yb	71 Lu
Actinides	89 Ac	90 Th	91 Pa	92 U	93 Np	94 Pu	95 Am	96 Cm	97 Bk	98 Cf	99 Es	100 Fm	101 Md	102 No	103 Lr

When you compare the elements against each other on a relative basis and ask the question, "Which of these two elements is a better choice to use as money?" the answer you arrive at will be the same one that mankind has reached repeatedly throughout history—gold. It meets all of Aristotle's criteria. The fact that it is also beautiful and easy to identify are additional plusses. Historically, gold was not only money in "this life," but throughout history the wealthy were buried with their gold so they would have money in the "next life."

The whole key to understanding why gold is such a highly desired alternative investment is that governments and civilizations come and go, but *human nature never changes*. To further illustrate, the next sections describe four of the hundreds of possible examples of the "country death spiral" discussed in Chapter 1. The names of the countries and centuries change, but the human nature exhibited is consistent.

Death Spiral Lydia

The first recorded (around 560 BC) example of a western country death spiral occurred in Lydia, a kingdom which was ruled by King Croesus. The kingdom had rich mines and produced high-quality coins that were made of gold and silver (1 gold coin = 15 silver coins). At first, the coins were very successful, and Lydia thrived as a trading center. The money issued by Lydia served the purposes for which money was intended. Then, unfortunately, the king started to spend more than he could collect in taxes. Nearing the end of the death spiral, the king attempted to stretch his tax dollars further by directing the mint to dilute new gold coins with silver. Of course, diluting the gold with silver changed the color of the coins and the people and the merchants noticed the new coins were lighter in color.

The people behaved rationally and, suspecting that something wasn't quite right with the newer coins, hoarded the older darker coins and spent the new lighter ones. This led to what was later described in Gresham's law; namely, bad money drove the good money out of the marketplace. The merchants were now only paid with the lighter coins and, believing them to be of lower value (although not sure why), raised their prices. This was the first recorded western example of monetary inflation.

The people complained to the king that prices were rising. This is, of course, the great irony. People complained to the government about higher prices, when it was the government that caused them.

Only the government can cause monetary inflation. First the king tried ordering the merchants not to raise prices (price controls), but the merchants ran out of goods. The king then instructed the mint to dilute the gold coins with darker metals (copper, bronze) in an attempt to hide the fact that the gold was being diluted. While this resulted in darker coins, the weight was wrong. As a result, no one trusted the coins, their value collapsed, the country's army scattered, and Lydia was soon conquered by Persia. The moral of the story? A key to a country's defense is maintaining the purchasing power of its currency!

Death Spiral Rome

Like Lydia, Rome was founded on the principle of hard money. However, by 60 BC the financial death cycle described in Chapter 1 was nearing completion. The country had exhausted its capacity to borrow and was rapidly debasing its currency by substituting cheaper metals and making smaller coins. The Roman Empire was on the verge of collapse. Then in 58 BC, Julius Caesar returned from his northern campaigns and brought back enough gold and silver to pay off Rome's debts. In addition, he was able to pay each of his soldiers 200 gold pieces—the ultimate economic stimulus program.

Rome was able to return to gold, copper, bronze, and primarily silver coins. As time progressed, however, and Rome's responsible rulers were replaced, human nature exerted itself again, and the financial death cycle returned:

- Octavian (31 BC) kept the silver content of the coins at 100%.
- Nero (AD 54) reduced the silver content from 100% to 90%.
- Trajan (AD 98) reduced the silver content from 90% to 85%.

- Marcus Aurelius (AD 161) reduced the silver content from 85% to 75%.
- Gallienus (AD 260) reduced the silver content from 75% to 4%.
- Diocletian (AD 301) issued the first "paper money" called denarii which were not backed by gold or other commodities (aka "fiat money").

Diocletian further issued an edict that required merchants not to shut down and to honor the paper as if it were real silver. In effect he increased the money supply at a faster rate than the economy grew. According to the laws of economics, this will result in inflation. With no limits on printing paper and just calling it money, Rome's rulers just kept printing it, and spending it, to buy the public's approval. The resulting inflation was spectacular:

- In AD 301, one pound of gold bought 25,000 denarii.
- By AD 302, one pound of gold bought 50,000 denarii.
- By AD 307, one pound of gold bought 100,000 denarii.
- By AD 324, one pound of gold bought 300,000 denarii.
- By AD 350, one pound of gold bought 2,000,000,000 denarii.

After AD 350, Rome couldn't pay its army enough to stay up with inflation. The soldiers began to desert en masse. Sixty years later in AD 410, Rome was defeated and the Dark Ages began. Human nature wins again.

Death Spiral France

When Louis XIV died in 1715, he left France 3 billion livres in debt—some of which was spent building the palace at Versailles.

Unfortunately, France only had tax revenue of 142 million livres. Since the new king, Louis XV, was only 7 years old, the Duc d'Orleans was appointed as the new king's regent. The Duc tried to deal with the debt by immediately ordering that the mint reduce the size of the coins by 20% and ordering that the smaller coins be accepted just like the existing larger coins: inflation and price controls in one step. The people responded logically by hoarding the larger coins and spending the new ones as fast as possible. A brief economic expansion and inflation ensued—but then fizzled. The state then offered rewards for the names of hoarders of the larger coins who, once identified, were promptly sent to the bastille. Despite the threat of prison, France suffered an acute shortage of gold coins in circulation.

Along came John Law, who proposed a radical solution. He would create a bank that would issue paper that supposedly was backed by gold coins. The advantage that the paper offered was that, in the highly probable event that the coins were again debased, the paper could still be converted into the pre-debased older coins. Because of this benefit many people were happy to deposit their gold and accept the paper. The bank could make this guarantee because it never expected to do any conversions. With no constraints on issuing paper, the bank lent far more "paper coins" than it had real coins in inventory. For a while, these paper coins were accepted and "papered over" the French government's shortage of real gold. The bank naturally issued far more paper than it collected gold, which effectively increased the money supply and allowed people to buy goods, build buildings, and pay taxes. The Duc was impressed and gave John Law's Bank additional rights.

One right he was given was the right to sell shares on the monopoly on trade with the French territories in the United States. The first shares sold at 550 livres and rose dramatically. Subsequent offerings were at much higher prices. People became rich—on paper. One depositor, Prince de Conti, upset that he was unable to buy all the stock he wanted during one of the secondary offerings, showed up at the bank with three wagons and demanded to exchange the bank's paper for gold coins. He got his three wagons, but the Duc convinced him to return two of them. This political "arm twisting" was interpreted as evidence that Law's bank didn't have enough gold coin to back its paper. The smart money started to cash in the paper with the bank or use them to buy gold, silver, and jewels, and immediately shipped them out of the country. Once a run started on the bank, the law was changed to prevent the ownership of gold and prohibit its removal from the state (currency controls). Financial collapse ensued. It took France generations to recover and its ruin allowed Napoleon to rise to power.

The cycle repeated again in France under Charlemagne, in Venice in AD 1382 under Contarini, in Spain in AD 1511 under Ferdinand, and hundreds of other civilizations that have come and gone throughout the history of the western world.

DEATH SPIRAL THE UNITED STATES

In 1760, when the United States was a British colony, four methods of payment were in common use:

- **Barter**—Particularly along the frontier, where the universe of "goods to buy" was limited, trappers would swap furs and bear teeth for guns, ammunition, frying pans, sugar, salt, new traps, and other necessities.
- **Warehouse receipts**—To create warehouse receipts, a farmer would take agriculture products such as tobacco, rice, live-

stock, or bales of cotton to a centralized warehouse. There, they were inspected for quality and approved. The farmer then swapped, for example, cotton bales for sheets of paper called receipts. Each receipt allowed the bearer to remove one bale of cotton from the warehouse at the convenience of the bearer. Armed with this "money" the farmer then went to the general store, the feed store, the livery, and the dress shop, and swapped the receipts for supplies. The warehouse receipts often traded hands many times before someone returned them to the warehouse and redeemed them for the cotton bales. Buying goods with paper warehouse receipts was easier than dragging around bales of cotton. This "money" got its value because it could be exchanged for a fixed quantity of a valuable commodity.

- **British pounds**—What is now the United States was a series of colonies and, particularly in the North, did a lot of trade with England. At the time, the pound was a warehouse receipt that was exchangeable for a fixed quantity of gold and so was similar to an agricultural receipt.

- **Gold and silver coins from around the world**—Because they were made of nearly pure gold or silver, it didn't matter whether coins were originally French, German, English, or Spanish. At this point, the colonies didn't produce their own coins. In fact, the most common gold coin in the colonies was the Spanish piece of eight. Local privateers (pirates) frequently raided Spanish shipping from Central and South America and stole the gold that the Spanish had stolen from the Incas. The privateers would return to port, spend the gold, and the money cascaded through the economy.

Then, the original 13 colonies declared independence from Britain. Of course, "declaring independence" and "obtaining independence" are two different things. The war of independence had to be financed. To this end, the colonies:

- Borrowed from its wealthy residents
- Borrowed from Britain's European enemies—especially France, the Netherlands, and Spain
- Printed its first currency, called the continental, in 1775, shown in Figure 3.2

FIGURE 3.2

Continentals

The continental was technically a debt instrument—not a warehouse receipt. They were supposed to be redeemed in silver with taxes collected after the war ended. To willingly accept continentals as payment, you had to believe that the colonies would:

- Win the war.
- Be able to collect enough in taxes to pay off its accumulated debt—after meeting its current expenses.

In short, continentals were the ultimate junk bonds, and few merchants accepted them willingly. Instead, the continental army would force people to take them as payment when it commandeered supplies. As the war dragged on year after year, more continentals were printed, leading to "printing press inflation." When the revolutionary war was finally won, the newly free country was so far in debt that there was no way it could ever pay it off. The fledgling country converted the continentals into new silver-backed dollars in 1792 at a rate of $1,000 in continentals for each $1.00 in new silver dollars. The new dollar was defined as a warehouse receipt that was fully exchangeable for 371¼ grains of silver. For the next 100 years, the worst insult you could hurl at someone was that they were as "worthless as a continental."

In order to protect the people from again being fleeced by the new government, the US constitution, in Article 1, Section 10, provided that "No state shall . . . make anything but gold and silver coin a tender in payment of debts." This unambiguous statement would seem to preclude not only any fiat currencies—but also government sponsored warehouse receipts. Note: This rule makes no provision against *private* entities—such as banks—issuing warehouse receipts for those who don't want to carry gold and silver coins.

The country continued with gold and silver dollars until the Civil War. Wars are very expensive, and the loser is usually the side that runs out of money first. Both the North and the South ran out of gold and silver and resorted to issuing fiat currencies. Figure 3.3 shows the Confederate fiat currency.

In 1861, the North issued "greenbacks," which the government declared were good for paying all obligations (wages, store purchases, and the like) except taxes. Taxes still had to be paid in gold and silver. Like continentals, the greenbacks were to be paid off in gold and silver from taxes collected after the war ended. They were, therefore, debt instruments whose value rose and fell as each battlefield report was received. If the North won a battle, the value of the greenbacks rose. If the North lost a battle, the value fell. Of course the North won the war and, in 1879, more than 14 years after the war ended, the last of the greenbacks were exchanged for gold or silver coins or for new currency warehouse receipts for gold and silver. The taxes to pay off the debt were collected primarily from the southern states as punishment for trying to secede.

FIGURE 3.3

Confederate Fiat Money

After the Civil War, backing for currencies around the globe switched from silver to gold because a flood of silver from the largest silver strike in history, the Comstock Lode in Virginia City, Nevada, hit the market. Again, the western world ran on gold (Figure 3.4).

FIGURE 3.4

US $50 Gold Receipt

In 1914, World War I began. Both sides in this European war traded with the United States, and the United States accumulated an incredibly large percentage of the world's gold. By 1917, the United States was the only major power still on the gold standard—the European countries had run out of gold and were borrowing and printing money in a desperate bid to survive. The United States entered the war and brought it to a quick close. After the war ended, the US economy exploded. Europe was in ruins, and the United States had unlimited labor and production capacity. In the late 1920s and early 1930s, the United States was like China in the 1990s—its economy was growing at a double-digit annual rate. US investors discovered leverage, and asset prices (especially common stock) soared to unrealistic levels. The bubble finally broke in 1929. However, at the time, unlike today, only the rich owned stocks, and so it took a while for the stock market crash to trickle down to Main Street.

By 1931, the economic slowdown hit Main Street, and some banks failed. People were no longer comfortable holding warehouse receipts that promised to be exchangeable for gold—they wanted the physical gold! Imagine their surprise when they found that the US government, like hundreds of governments before it, had printed up more warehouse receipts (Figure 3.5) than it had in actual gold. The government did this so that it could spend more than it was able to collect in taxes.

FIGURE 3.5

US $20 Gold Receipt

In 1933, to avoid a run on the banks, Roosevelt closed the banks and confiscated all privately held gold bullion. Figure 3.6 shows Roosevelt's order to deliver all gold coin, gold bullion, and gold certificates to a Federal Reserve Bank. Penalties for noncompliance included a fine of up to $10,000 and up to 10 years in prison. (Exceptions were granted for foreigners, religious medallions, and rare coins.) The grab brought in $500 million in gold. People who owned gold in bank gold certificates lost it; people who held gold at home often simply buried it in the backyard.

When the government confiscated the gold, it paid citizens the official exchange rate of $20.67 an ounce in paper currency. After it completed the confiscation, the government then raised the price of gold—devalued the dollar—to $35 an ounce. As President Obama's chief of staff Rahm Emanuel said, "You never want a serious crisis to go to waste." In this crisis, the government effectively seized 40% of many high-net-worth individuals' wealth. This is also when the United States defaulted. US money went from being a warehouse receipt exchangeable for gold to a green piece of paper in the world's largest Ponzi scheme. It is always amusing when someone asks, "Can the United States really default?" The answer is, "It already has!" It promised to pay in gold and then reneged on the promise. That is a default by anyone's definition.

FIGURE 3.6

Roosevelt's Order to Confiscate Gold

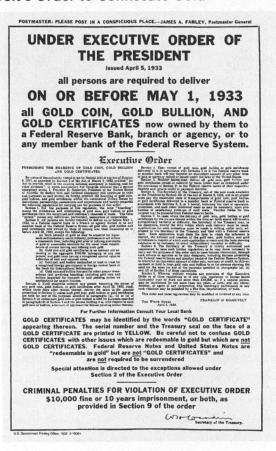

After WWII, the Marshall Plan was designed to expedite Germany's and Japan's recovery. Part of this plan was the Bretton Woods agreement, which gave Germany new "Marks" and Japan new "Yen" to replace their previous ones which were worthless when the war ended. These new currencies were given a fixed exchange rate for the US dollar, which itself had a fixed exchange rate for gold (only for foreigners). It was this link to gold, once removed, that gave these new currencies instant value and credibility.

As the world bought US goods and US companies expanded around the globe, the economy grew so quickly that the country was able to significantly pay down (as a percentage of GDP) its World War II debt.

Then came the 1950s, '60s, '70s. A new generation took over and wanted both guns and butter. On the gun side, the United States was fighting a very expensive and unpopular war in Vietnam, as well as the Cold War. The hawks didn't want to raise taxes to pay for the war because that would raise opposition to it. On the butter side, the United States added a plethora of new social programs, including Medicaid, Medicare, student loans, federal housing, food stamps, and social security adjustments for inflation, but assessed no taxes to pay for them. By now the world was catching up with the United States. Europe was rebuilt and turning out high-quality goods. Asia exploded, first with cheap goods—but then with ever more complex goods. With new competition, the US economy no longer grew fast enough to allow increases in spending without higher taxes. Democrats wouldn't cut spending, Republicans wouldn't raise taxes, so the country started to run up huge deficits, which it financed by issuing debt.

The country also began to print money—in the process moving from a full reserve system where every dollar in circulation was backed by gold to a fractional reserve system where each dollar was only partially backed by gold. Going from a full to a partial reserve system by printing money created monetary inflation—and the price of commodities (including gold and silver) soared.

In 1964, the United States resorted to one of the most dramatic steps on the "slide to economic ruin." The US government debased its currency by no longer issuing quarters and dimes that were composed of 90% silver. Instead, the new quarters and dimes were only silver plated. The government did this because the value of the silver in the pre-1964 coins exceeded to face value of the coin. In other words, you could buy four silver quarters for $1.00, melt the quarters, and sell the silver for more than $1.00—a risk-free arbitrage.

France, and then other European countries, realized there were more paper dollars than gold to back them, and so they did the obvious arbitrage: they bought paper dollars and sent them to the United States for gold. On August 15, 1971, Nixon devalued the dollar to $37 per ounce of gold, and then later to $42 per ounce of gold to make the paper–gold arbitrage less attractive. It was no use. The demand to swap paper for metal continued, and it became obvious that the United States would lose all of its gold unless it did something. Nixon did. He closed the gold window and eliminated the right of foreigners to exchange paper dollars for gold. This was the second phase of the modern US default.

With the gold window closed, there was now no limit on how much currency the government could print—and it began to print with a vengeance. President Ford again allowed investors to buy gold and its value quickly rose from $175 an ounce to $850 an ounce as a hedge against the inevitable monetary inflation that accompanies money printing. The price rose to $850 because, at the time, if you divided the number of dollars in the money supply by the number of ounces of gold owned by the United States, you came up with an exchange rate of about $850 per ounce.

Fortunately, just before we got to the point of no return, Carter appointed Paul Volcker as Fed Chairman. Volcker started to shrink the number of dollars in order to support their value. (Note the analogy to Caesar returning to Rome and giving Rome a second chance to get it right.) Because of the law of supply and demand, reducing the number of dollars increased the cost of borrowing those dollars, and interest rates rose to levels the United States hadn't seen since the Civil War. With T-bills yielding almost 16% and offering a real return of 6% (16% – 10% inflation), holding gold became very expensive and the price started to drop, eventually reaching a low of $252. This was below the cost of mining, and so the mines temporarily shut down. This is significant. If the price of gold drops below the cost of producing it, then gold production stops. This helps maintain the balance between supply and demand.

Reagan then crushed the Soviet Union by outspending them and left the United States as the world's sole superpower. Since the United States was the world's sole superpower, everyone wanted to hold its currency and our government obliged them by printing dollars night and day. It seemed every family around the world elected to hold some of their savings in paper US dollars. They gave the United States oil, textiles, labor, and raw materials, and the United States gave them green paper. A great deal for the United States!

The BRIC's (Brazil, Russia, India, and China) rapidly expanding economies also accumulated reserves. A large portion of the reserves were invested in US debt. Those reserve funds acted as "sponges" to absorb the unprecedented levels of debt the United States was issuing. Lastly, until 2010, the Social Security Trust Fund also acted as a sponge in that it brought more dollars in than it sent out. By law, the surplus was invested in US Treasuries. The net result of the sole superpower status and the sponges was that the United States was able to issue trillions in debt (on and off balance sheet) at ridiculously low interest rates. The money from the sale of debt was used to provide services to US residents and compensation to public employees that were way beyond the government's ability to provide via taxation. The excess cash resulted first in a massive tech stock bubble and later a huge US real estate bubble.

Two events accelerated the United States to the verge of collapse: the 9/11 attack and the bursting of the real estate bubble. The two wars (Iraq and Afghanistan) that followed the 9/11 attack cost the United States almost $1 trillion. The collapse of the US real estate market looked like it was going to bring down the banking system—not just in the United States, but throughout the world. Banks around the world held vast quantities of US mortgage-backed securities, as well as loans to US banks. The crises quickly spread to insurance companies, pension plans, and individuals who owned US mortgages indirectly via mutual funds and mortgage backed securities.

The Fed reacted to the mortgage crisis with levels of intervention that were unprecedented in the history of the world. At its peak, the Fed temporarily extended $16 trillion of credit to institutions all over the world and a complete collapse was averted—or, perhaps more precisely, postponed. Almost all of this money has been repaid and the Fed deserves high praise for its bold actions at the height of the crisis to prevent an uncontrolled, unmanaged economic collapse. However, since then, the Fed has abandoned its primary mission (which is to protect the value of the dollar) and has been overly concerned with stimulating the economy instead of allowing the economy to cleanse itself. Economic crashes are like forest fires—they are very destructive, but necessary occasionally to clean out the excessive undergrowth and allow the forest to regrow in a healthier state. The Fed should have helped ensure that the crash was orderly, or at least as orderly as possible, but it should not be trying to fight the need for a crash. By attempting to do so, the Fed is only making the eventual and inevitable collapse worse.

CHAPTER FOUR

The US Death Spiral Accelerates

The US federal government has, step by step, implemented the death spiral and the pace of decay is rapidly accelerating. The federal government, as well as the state and some local governments, started the spiral by excessive spending, and then kicking the can down the road, imposing crony capitalism, creating off balance sheet debt, delaying maintenance, mismanaging natural resources, raiding trust accounts, and seizing private property without compensation. In short, the US government is following the historical path to economic collapse. Let's review recent US history.

BORROWING MONEY TO MEET CURRENT OPERATIONAL EXPENSES

- In 2009, the United States borrowed approximately $1.6 trillion. The human brain is not designed to be able to visualize a number that large. To help visualize it, the deficit for this one year was equal to the entire economy of Canada. Thus, in 2009 alone, the United States "borrowed Canada" to make up the shortfall between its tax collections and its expenses.

- In 2010, the United States borrowed approximately $1.4 trillion.
- In 2011, the United States borrowed approximately $1.3 trillion.
- In 2012, the United States borrowed approximately $1.3 trillion.
- In 2013 and beyond, the Congressional Budget Office projects the annual deficits for the next 5 years to be near $1 trillion (exclusive of one-time events such as the massive influx of taxes in advance of the capital gains tax rates rising). In other words, unless Congress undertakes extreme measures to cut spending and raise revenue, the "on the books" debt will rise to $20+ trillion. Obviously, this is more than the United States can ever expect to repay without seriously debasing its currency. Figure 4.1 and Figure 4.2 provide visual representations of the debt trend projected through fiscal year 2016 and 2017, respectively, and show that the blame is equally shared among both major parties. Once exponential growth of debt starts, it's very hard to reverse.

FIGURE 4.1

Gross Public Debt

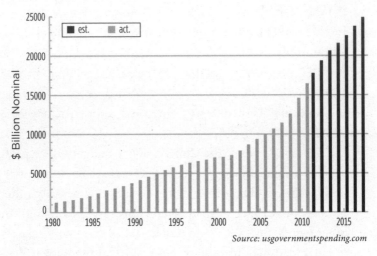

Source: usgovernmentspending.com

It makes no difference who controls Congress:

- 1977–1980 Democrats
- 1981–1986 split
- 1987–1994 Democrats
- 1995–1996 split
- 1997–2002 Republicans
- 2003–2004 split
- 2005–2006 Republicans
- 2007–2010 Democrats
- 2011–2014 split

The only reason the United States hasn't had significant problems servicing its debt so far is that interest rates have been declining, making the total cost of servicing the ever increasing debt fairly constant. The ever increasing debt principal has been largely offset by a lower average interest payment on that debt. Obama has been given a free ride on debt since the interest rates have been at record lows. The Fed expects interest rates will rise—but not until 2015. If the average rate on its debt were to rise to 8%, interest alone in 2016 will be greater than $1.6 trillion. Federal tax revenue (excluding Social Security) from all sources is about $4.5 trillion, so by 2017, just paying the interest on the debt might take 33% of federal revenue. Figure 4.2 shows the US debt as a percentage of the gross domestic product from 1792 through 2012. Note the spikes in debt ties to wars.

FIGURE 4.2

US Debt as a Percentage of GDP

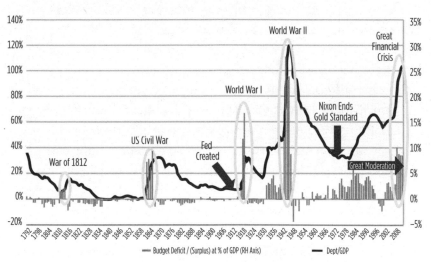

Source: usgovernmentspending.com

POSTPONING THE
RECOGNITION OF EXPENSES

If only governments followed the rules they make the rest of us follow. In the United States, all private pension plans are required by the government to fund their plans as the employees earn benefits. Each year the employee works, the company has to put money into the plan to pay the retirement income and health benefits the employee accrues during that year. The money is held at a trust company, so the employee's retirement benefits are secured—from the employer.

Federal employees have been promised extremely generous pensions (by private employer standards), as well as health care for life. Unfortunately, not one penny has been set aside in a segregated trust to pay for the pensions or health benefits of federal employees. These benefits are paid out of current tax revenue. An entire wave of federal employees is just starting to retire. This will raise the costs of the federal government substantially, even if there is a freeze on the size of the federal work force.

Obviously, these overly generous retirement benefits are going to have to be substantially reduced in the future. The country simply can't afford them. The Association of Federal State County and Municipal Employees (AFSCME) were represented in their negotiations by some of the country's best lawyers. They could have negotiated for a funded trust account and current funding of their future benefits. They didn't because they knew that would have caused taxes to skyrocket. If taxes skyrocketed, the people would want to know why. That would attract too much unwanted attention on the excessive benefit levels, and they would have been reduced. Instead, the union primarily negotiated higher pay and job security for its members and rolled the dice that the future generations would be both willing and able to pay their retirement benefits. That roll may come up snake eyes.

Engaging in Pay to Play/Crony Capitalism

In the United States, both political parties have large contributors (GOP—oil, pharmaceutical, defense, the NRA, and agriculture; DEM—unions, alternative energy, autos, and banking). These contributors expect a return on their investment when the party they back with their dollars wins. That return on investment can take the form of regulatory changes, research grants, changes in tariffs, access to federally owned lands and resources, federal contracts, federal bailouts, a free pass on criminal prosecution for corporate wrongdoing, and/or permission to export high tech equipment.

In the most recent example, the Obama administration has taken heat for giving Solyndra, a US solar panel producer, a huge federally guaranteed loan right before it went bankrupt. The owners of Solyndra were big contributors to Obama's campaign. This loan became more embarrassing for the administration when it became apparent that:

- Every private financing source rejected Solyndra because its products were obsolete and its business model was unworkable. To even a semi-skilled junior analyst, it was obvious the company was going to be a failure.
- The rules for vetting and approving the federal loan were circumvented and internal warnings that any new financing would be money down a rat hole were ignored or overruled.
- The loan was subordinated to other loans the company had received in direct violation of the rules for federal loans.

The US taxpayers who funded this loan lost 100% of their investment. Despite the clear policy violations, there was no serious investigation; no prosecution for rules violation, no one in the government even lost their job. The taxpayers were fleeced for $850 million. As of this writing, the Obama administration insists on $30 billion of additional stimulus money to spread around to supporters as part of an agreement to avoid the fiscal cliff.

As an example of the decline in the quality of government servant, consider the difference between President Truman and Speaker Pelosi. As president, Harry Truman paid for his own meals and travel expenses. When he left office in 1953, he and his wife drove home to Missouri by themselves. There was no Secret Service following them. His only income was a US Army pension reported to have been $13,507.72 a year and an "allowance" granted by Congress. Later, noting that he paid for his stamps and personally licked them, Congress granted him a retroactive pension of $25,000 per year.

When offered corporate positions at large salaries, Truman declined, stating, "I turned down all of those offers. I knew that they were not interested in hiring Harry Truman, the person, but what they wanted to hire was the former President of the United States. I could never lend myself to any transaction, however respectable, that would commercialize on the prestige and the dignity of the office of the Presidency."

On May 6, 1971, when Congress was preparing to award him the Medal of Honor on his 87th birthday, he refused to accept it, writing, "I don't consider that I have done anything which should be the reason for any award, Congressional or otherwise."

When he died, his only asset was his house in Independence, Missouri, which his wife had inherited from her mother and father. Other than their years in the White House, they lived their entire lives there.

Modern politicians, on the other hand, have found a new level of success in cashing in on being in the government. Today, many in Congress have also found a way to become quite wealthy while enjoying the fruits of their offices. Compare the above true public service of Truman to Nancy Pelosi, who as Speaker of the House was provided secure transportation by military aircraft for official business. As a result of a Freedom of Information Act request filed by Judicial Watch, the US Air Force released documents detailing Pelosi's use of USAF aircraft between March 2009 and June 2010. Here are the main highlights revealed by the USAF:

Several flights included Ms. Pelosi's guests, such as grown children, grandchildren, and various in-laws, friends, and hangers-on, and more than 95% of the trips were between the West Coast and Washington, DC. They found that she took 85 trips over a 68-week period, or an average of 1.25 trips per week, with a total mileage of 206,264 miles, or 2,427 average miles per trip. The total flying time was 428.6 hours, or an average of 5 hours per trip. The cost to the taxpayers was $2,100,744, or $27,715 per trip. The cost of in-flight food and alcohol alone was $101,429, or $1,193 per trip.

In the recent 2.5% across-the-board sequestration, some departments, instead of trying to minimize the impact on the public, seemed to go out of their way to implement the cuts in such a way as to maximize the impact on the public. The FAA, instead of sequestering managers in Washington, went straight for the nation's jugular—the air traffic controllers. Fortunately, the people's outrage caused the FAA to retreat. The sheer audacity of an agency that works for us assuming it could "punish us" for cutting its funding suggests a government that is out of control.

INCREASING OFF BALANCE SHEET DEBT

In addition to huge direct borrowing, the United States also has numerous agencies that have issued their own debt. The justification for this agency debt not being on the US balance sheet is that the debt is not guaranteed by the full faith and credit of the United States. Instead, it is guaranteed only by the agency that issued it and the moral guarantee of the United States. This is a bit of hair splitting; if any of these agencies were to fail, they would bring the entire financial system down. Therefore, even if they aren't backed by the full faith and credit of the United States, they have to be bailed out, and when necessary, they have been. These agencies have, collectively, borrowed over $10 trillion. This makes the US debt not $16 trillion on its way to $20 trillion—but $26 trillion on its way to $30 trillion. Some of the major agencies are:

- Government National Mortgage Association (GNMA) aka Ginnie Mae
- Federal National Mortgage Association (FNMA) aka Fannie Mae
- Federal Home Loan Mortgage Corporation (FHLMC) aka Freddie Mac
- Federal Farm Credit Bank
- Federal Home Loan Bank
- SLM Corporation (commonly known as Sallie Mae, originally the Student Loan Marketing Association)
- Tennessee Valley Authority (TVA)

Without a government bailout both Fannie Mae and Freddie Mac would have defaulted. While the government has guaranteed their debt, it has not moved their debt to its own balance sheet. This is a clear and intentional violation of the most basic accounting conventions. Part one of solving a problem is admitting it. By continuing to keep this agency debt off the US balance sheet, Washington is clearly stating that it has no interest in honestly dealing with its citizens about its problems.

Delaying Maintenance of Assets

The United States has 151,394 bridges that are deemed obsolete or unsafe. Our public railroads in the Northeast are a global embarrassment and our east coast port facilities were obsolete 30 years ago. Our highways are too small to handle the traffic; traffic jams cost hundreds of billions of dollars in wasted time and fuel—not to mention the environmental cost. Likewise, the capacity of our airports has not come close to keeping pace with increases in air travel. The electric grid in much of the country is above ground and relies on equipment that is well past its expected retirement date.

These are disasters waiting to happen. It's not a question of if, but when, another major bridge will collapse like the recent collapse of the I-35 bridge over the Mississippi River and the I-5 bridge in Washington. Likewise, whether it is taken down by solar flares, a terrorist attack, or a violent storm, our electric grid is way too vulnerable. Estimates of the cost of fixing our infrastructure run from $3 trillion to $5 trillion—money we don't have because we wasted it on an ever-growing bloated bureaucracy and misguided projects.

For example, in a well-intended but poorly implemented attempt to achieve energy independence, the United States requires that gasoline be mixed with ethanol. In the United States, we make ethanol from corn in a very inefficient process. It takes approximately a gallon of gas (some experts say more than a gallon) and more than ten gallons of water to make a gallon of ethanol. In addition, making ethanol consumes 40% of the US corn crop—causing the price of corn to soar globally. Given that the United States is awash in natural gas, we would be better off tapping the gas and using the corn and water to feed the world and quench its growing thirst.

RAIDING TRUST FUNDS

In addition to kicking liabilities down the road, the US government has raided every trust fund its tentacles can penetrate. The government has approximately 230 trust funds, including Medicare, Social Security (SS), Social Security's Supplemental Security Income (SSI), and the Highway Trust Fund, to name a few. However, instead of these trust funds being full of stocks, corporate bonds, gold, and CDs, like private trust accounts, they are full of US Treasury IOUs.

As soon as money is paid into the trusts, the US government pulls it out and replaces it with Treasury IOUs. The government then spends the money on current expenses. The late Senator Daniel Moynihan called this "outright thievery." For example, until recently, the Social Security Trust Fund was a significant source of funding for the government since the fund received far more money in contributions than was paid out in benefits—leaving a surplus that could be borrowed. That changed in 2011 when the Social Security Trust Fund paid out more in benefits than it collected. In 2012, the net withdrawals equaled $47.8 billion. This net withdrawal phase wasn't supposed to happen until 2020, but the combination of high unemployment and reduction in wages caused:

- More workers to elect to receive benefits at age 62.
- Fewer workers to make contributions.
- Many workers to make smaller contributions.

In addition, the trust earns a low interest rate on the Treasuries in its portfolio. The fund's trustees assumed the portfolio would yield 4%, but the new Treasuries the fund is adding yield less. As a result, unless changes are made, the fund will not be able to pay 100% of promised benefits starting in 2040. That 2040 date will fluctuate based upon how well the economy does. To repair the program will require some combination of the following:

- Raising taxes on current workers. There used to be five workers per retiree. Thus, if benefits were raised, the cost of one retiree's increase was spread over five workers. Today that number is only 1.67 workers per retiree. Obviously, paying for these benefits is a greater burden on today's young.
- Means testing. Those retirees with wealth, or income, above a certain level would not receive full benefits. This turns the program into a welfare program.
- Gradually increase the retirement age to offset the increase in longevity—a rational solution.
- Reduce the cost of living adjustment to one-half the real increase—another rational solution.

When the premiums were set for Medicare years ago, few anticipated that people would live so long and that medical science would make so many exciting, but expensive, advances. As a result, the Medicare Trust Fund simply doesn't have enough money to provide state-of-the-art care for the elderly for life. The current retirees simply didn't pay enough into the trust fund to provide the benefits they now receive. It is simple math. Now, the AARP argues that people paid for their benefits and are entitled to receive them. No objection. But they paid enough in to lease a Ford Focus for five years and now want a BMW 7 Series for ten years. It can't be done for the same money. Congress's only answer to date has been to pay doctors and hospitals less while increasing their regulatory and liability burdens—a not a viable long-term strategy.

Again, the age should be gradually raised and a limit should be placed on both annual and lifetime benefits. Some will argue that this places a value on human life—which is true—but we do that all the time. We could make a car that was so safe that you would never get hurt in an accident. Of course, the car would be so expensive no one could buy it. So, we accept the trade-off of an affordable car for a reasonable risk of death/injury while driving. Medicare would become an affordable program which would meet the complete needs of 95 out of 100 retirees. Those who wanted to could buy a catastrophic policy privately to protect them if they end up in the 5% that required additional medical care beyond their Medicare limits.

DEBASE THE MONEY

One of the last stages of a country's decline is to simply print money. As of the start of 2013, the Federal Reserve Bank is buying 90% of the New Treasuries being issued and is just printing the money required to buy them. This is in addition to the $40 billion a month the Fed is printing to buy mortgage-backed securities. Since the financial crisis began, the Fed has purchased more than $3 trillion of mortgages and Treasuries by simply printing money. Figure 4.3 shows the increase in the US money supply. The Fed expects this to increase to at least $5 trillion before it stops buying—and starts selling. This assumes the economy recovers by 2014. If not, all bets are off and the Fed may simply keep buying. By the law of supply and demand, as the number of dollars increases, their value declines—especially when the number of dollars is increasing in an economy that's fairly stagnant. Figure 4.4 illustrates this decreasing purchasing power.

FIGURE 4.3

Increase in the Money Base

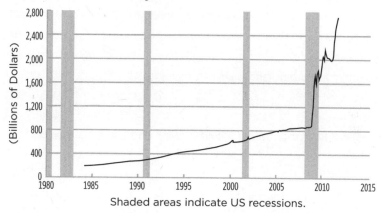

Shaded areas indicate US recessions.

Source: Federal Reserve Bank of St. Louis

FIGURE 4.4

Decline in the Purchasing Power of the Dollar

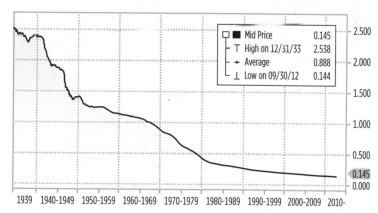

Source: Bloomberg

Over the last 10 years, the decline in purchasing power has been especially obvious in the shrinking packages of consumer goods. A can of coffee once contained a pound, then 14 ounces, and now fewer than 12 ounces. Packages of cereal, cake mixes, mixed nuts, tissues, and so forth, have all gotten smaller while the price stayed the same or rose. Particularly aggravating is Pillsbury cake mix, which used to make 24 cupcakes but now makes 20. Cupcake pans, however, are designed for 12 or 24. Every trip to the supermarket becomes more painful, as shown in Figure 4.5.

FIGURE 4.5

Decline in Purchasing Power over the Last 10 Years

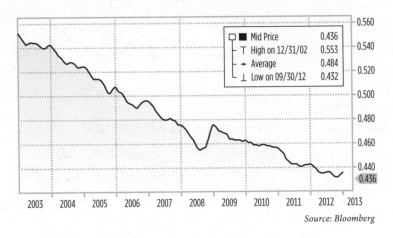

Source: Bloomberg

THREE BURNING FUSES

The first burning fuse is the aging of the baby boom generation. In addition to Social Security and Medicare (discussed earlier in this chapter), there is a third entitlement—disability payments. As people get older, they are more likely to become disabled. Adding to the magnitude of this time bomb is the fact that many who are losing their jobs in their mid to late 50s realize that they may never have a real job again. After exhausting their unemployment benefits—including the extended benefits—they are desperate to secure another source of income. Some are resorting to faking or, at the very least, exaggerating the extent of their disabilities.

Helping them game the system is a battery of attorneys—the ones who run late night ads with low production values. With the help of attorneys, people are filing and winning disability claims for dermatitis, stress, carpal tunnel syndrome, adult ADD, and the like. Since claims citing these clauses were never anticipated, they were not priced into the premiums workers paid. So again, the current generation about to retire underpaid for the benefits they are now asking to receive. The number of people on disability during George Bush's last term started at 5,067,119 and reached 7,442,377 at the end. During Obama's first term, that number reached 8,442,377—and is growing at a rate of 45,000 per month. As of December 2012, the number was 8,827,795. As of May 7, 2013, 10,962,532 people were collecting disability benefits. At this rate the number will hit 15 million well before the end of Obama's second term. That's 1 out of 25 Americans on disability, or more importantly, 1 in every 10 workers.

Illegal Immigration

The second burning fuse in the United States is undocumented immigration. Much is made of the fact that we are a nation of immigrants. For that reason, it is supposedly un-American or selfish to want to restrict immigration since, with the exception of Native Americans, we are all descended from immigrants at some point in the past. Proponents for open borders say it is not fair to come here and then "close the door behind you." Proponents of immigration cite the famous quote from the poem found on the Statue of Liberty; "Give me your tired, your poor, your huddled masses yearning to breathe free, the wretched refuse of your teeming shore. Send these, the homeless, tempest-tossed to me; I lift my lamp beside the golden door!"

This is nonsense. In the past, the United States didn't adopt liberal immigration policies to be altruistic; these policies were adopted because they were in the country's best interest. Initially, we needed immigrants to populate and secure the land. The United States was a vast land and to grab and hold it, it needed to be populated. In the war of 1812, recent immigrants made up a significant portion of our troops. During the Industrial Revolution, we needed millions of unskilled and semi-skilled workers for our factories, mines, farms, and construction companies. In the 1910s and '20s, severe shortages of workers justified a very liberal immigration policy. During World War I and World War II, the United States had a virtually unlimited need for people to fight overseas and produce war goods at home so again immigrants were needed.

At the end of WWII, the door to immigrants was largely closed because we didn't need additional labor. The troops were home and needed jobs. Also, it takes time for immigrants to become Americans. They need to learn the language, laws, and customs. They need to become comfortable enough in the United States to leave the areas concentrated with fellow immigrants and spread throughout the country as a whole.

Prior to the 1950s, there was little or no safety net for the poor (unless they were veterans) so immigrants didn't receive much in government services. Even immigrants with children were inexpensive to society because the cost of primary education was quite low. As a result, immigrants often became net contributors to the United States within six months of arrival. They provided more benefit in work and taxes than they consumed in government services. Knowing that there was no safety net, the only immigrants attracted to the United States were the ones who looked for the opportunity to make a better life for themselves and their families and were willing to work for it.

This all changed with the technological revolution, the end of the Cold War, and the rise of global supply chains. Instead of needing large numbers of unskilled workers, the United States now has a large surplus of unskilled workers. Instead of it taking 5,000 strong men to staff a steel plant, it now takes 250 highly educated ones to man and maintain the computer terminals and robots. US citizens find themselves losing jobs to undocumented immigrants who underprice them.

In addition, undocumented immigrants now receive food and housing subsidies; income tax credits; free health care; and far more expensive primary, secondary, and college educations. The courts have consistently ruled that the children of illegal immigrants are entitled to the full range of social services provided to the children of US citizens. On one hand, the United States says, "Keep out!" but on the other hand, "If you do sneak in, you get a whole basket of goodies." This creates an irresistible temptation. Clearly, the United States is sending a mixed message.

The number of Hispanic immigrants has become so high that some no longer feel any pressure to assimilate. Why bother to learn to speak English when:

- Everyone around you speaks Spanish.
- There are a dozen TV stations broadcasting in Spanish.
- Most telephone greetings begin with "Press 1 for English. Press 2 for Spanish."
- Government forms are printed in many languages.

Refusing to assimilate is counterproductive for the immigrant and incredibly disrespectful to the host nation. Natural born citizens now are routinely denied jobs—particularly government jobs, because they aren't bilingual and able to service a population that shouldn't even be here.

On top of having to offer support and print documents in Spanish is the astronomical cost of tracking down, prosecuting, and deporting illegal immigrants—that is, when the justice department decides to actually do its sworn duty and enforce the law of the land. Because of these high costs, while most immigrants (legal and otherwise) will eventually become net contributors to the United States, it now may take decades. In the meantime, they impose a high net cost on society. The cost of providing ±11 million illegal immigrants with free health care and education while the immigrants are on the J-curve to becoming net contributors is overwhelming the country's schools, hospitals, and low income housing stock.

As further proof of the immigration insanity in Washington, while the United States suffers from an acute shortage of engineers, our graduate schools turn out the best in the world and then deport them back to their own countries instead of awarding them green cards with their diplomas.

Student Loans

The third burning fuse is student loans. The cost of a college education has increased at twice the rate of inflation for no good reason other than the government subsidizes it. As a result, the size of student loan balances has exploded to approximately $1 trillion. This amount now exceeds charge card balances. The problem is that, in this current downturn, 20% of recent college graduates are either unemployed or grossly underemployed, making timely repayments nearly impossible. Presently, the 90+ day default rate is 11%, an all time high. The unpaid interest is accruing on the recipient's balance sheet, thus raising their unpaid balance and future payments, or at the issuing bank, raising the chance of yet another bank failure. The bottom line is that every late payment raises the liabilities on a balance sheet somewhere.

POLITICAL GRIDLOCK

The US Pledge of Allegiance includes the phrase "One nation, under God, indivisible." Sadly, nothing could be further from the case. The United States is more divided today that at any time since the Civil War. The hottest-selling bumper sticker in Texas reads, "Secede." We are divided nearly 50-50 with two very different and wholly incompatible views of how our country should function.

On the one hand are the blue states that want a very large and strong central government. They want a cradle-to-grave national safety net and are usually in favor of very high individual, corporate, and estate tax rates, wealth transfer, and a high level of government regulation.

The red states on the other hand are primarily populated by people who want a small federal government—and, in fact, want very light government over all. They believe in self-sufficiency, that each state should set its own rules, and that people should choose to live in whatever state best matches their own point of view. They point to Massachusetts and New Hampshire.

The people in Massachusetts desire a high level of government services and are willing to pay for them—hence the state's nickname "taxachusetts." The majority of people in New Hampshire want a low level of services and low taxes—to the point that many roads in New Hampshire aren't even paved. Yet, the states exist side by side without real issues. By leaving most issues to the states, both blue and red state residents would have fewer conflicts. Each state would decide the most controversial social issues for its own citizens: same sex marriage, abortion rights, rent control, the right to carry handguns, acceptable immigration numbers and standards, and so on. Every citizen could live in a state that reflected his or her personal beliefs. Much of the conflict we experience today is because both sides feel the other is trying to impose their will on them.

The worst case scenario is what we have today, a 50-50 standoff. At least if one side won decisively, half the people would be happy. Today *no one is happy*—the public's rating of Congress reflects this.

SEIZING PRIVATE PROPERTY

The government is allowed to seize property for a *public purpose* provided it *pays fair compensation*. This is necessary so that one person doesn't hold up the construction of a highway that will benefit millions. However, the government is increasingly ignoring both requirements of the property seizure rules. This started on a large scale with the Clean Water Act. With the stroke of a pen, the government prohibited building on wide swathes of privately owned coastal land. Property owners who planned on building their homes or retirement homes on their lots were denied the use of their property. Those who bought land as investments suddenly saw the value of their lots plunge. After all, what is the value of a piece of land on which the owner can't build? Lots that were worth $500K+ became worthless—or worse, they became liabilities because the owners still had to pay property taxes on the land and pay any loans they took out to buy the land.

The government said protecting the wetlands was so important to the entire population that it justified the cost. That may be true. But then that cost should be paid by all of society—not just the people who happened to own the affected land. However, the government determined it would cost too much money to buy all the affected properties at fair market value, so it simply ignored its obligation to pay fair compensation by arguing that a zoning change wasn't a change of title and, therefore, no compensation was warranted. A "taking" by any other name is still a "taking."

In addition to impacting the value of property by changing zoning, the federal government can sometimes "legally" seize private property. The government started by seizing the proceeds of drug deals as a way of discouraging them. Its rules then expanded to allow the government to seize cars that have drugs in them. Lend your car to a friend who buys a few ounces of pot for personal use and you could lose your car. There are now cases where the federal government has seized entire hotels if there are drug deals going down in a few rooms. How is a desk clerk supposed to know what the guests are going to do in their rented room? Since when is it the desk clerk's responsibility to police activity in the rooms people rent?

There are now more than 400 federal offenses and thousands of state and local offenses for which your cash, car, bank accounts, and home can be seized—including shoplifting, hiring an illegal alien such as a maid (California), playing a car stereo too loud (New York), transporting illegal fireworks, gambling, having illegal drugs on your property, and merely discussing violating any law ("conspiracy"), such as underpaying your taxes. The law can be found at USCIS.gov, but the next page gives a summary from AmericanPatrol.com:

Section 274 Felonies Under the Federal Immigration and Nationality Act, INA 274A(A)(1)(A):

A person (including a group of persons, business, organization, or local government) commits a federal felony when she or he:

- assists an alien s/he should reasonably know is illegally in the U.S. or who lacks employment authorization, by transporting, sheltering, or assisting him or her to obtain employment, or
- encourages that alien to remain in the U.S. by referring him or her to an employer or by acting as employer or agent for an employer in any way, or
- knowingly assists illegal aliens due to personal convictions.

Penalties upon conviction include criminal fines, imprisonment, and forfeiture of vehicles and real property used to commit the crime. Aliens and employers violating immigration laws are subject to arrest, detention, and seizure of their vehicles or property. In addition, individuals or entities who engage in racketeering enterprises that commit (or conspire to commit) immigration-related felonies are subject to private civil suits for treble damages and injunctive relief.

More than $1 billion in property is now seized without trial each year, according to FEAR (Forfeiture Endangers American Rights), a national forfeiture defense organization. Once police seize your property, the burden of proof is on the property owner to prove the property's innocence. Any suspected illegal actions of your relatives, guests, friends, and employees on or even near your property are sufficient grounds to seize it.

In 1991, the Montgomery, Alabama, police seized the home of

69-year-old Gussie Mae Gantt after videotaping police informants buying drugs in her yard. Ms. Gantt had previously called the police, complaining about drug dealing in her neighborhood, and had posted no-trespassing signs, but the drug dealers ignored them. Police waited until there was a drug deal in her yard, and then seized her home.

Lastly, today the government seizes private property for private as well as public purposes. Homeowners with oceanfront property can have it seized so that the land can be sold to a hotel developer who will pay higher taxes. This reduces the definition of private property to a joke. Your property is yours only until the government can make more from it by taking it away from you and giving it to someone else.

Last Step: Currency Controls

The last step in a country's death spiral is to impose currency controls so that people who leave can't take their wealth with them, and people who stay can't convert their currency into another currency at the fair market rate. Unlike some countries, the United States taxes its citizens on income regardless of where they earn it. Further, US citizens are discouraged from having foreign bank accounts by increased reporting requirements and the knowledge that having overseas accounts results in increased IRS scrutiny. The government has also increased the reporting requirements on foreign institutions that have accounts from US citizens to the point where most foreign institutions refuse to accept US customers. While there are no currency controls yet, traveling with large quantities of cash or even buying a train ticket with cash will often invite unwanted and unwarranted police scrutiny.

CHAPTER FIVE

Is the United States Past the Point of No Return?

Given all of the issues we've discussed thus far and knowing where we are on the death spiral, can the United States get back to a balanced budget—or more precisely a budget surplus—so that it can start paying down its debt? Is there another Volcker out there who will reverse the money printing and instead shrink the number of dollars to the number that existed before the financial crisis—and then only increase the money supply in line with economic growth? Or, is the United State's currency death spiral so far along that the country is past the point of no return?

When a country is deeply in debt and that debt is growing exponentially, there are only four ways to attack the problem: raise taxes, cut spending, print money, and sell assets.

Raising Taxes

Even the most fervent libertarian wants some level of government and that government has to be paid for with taxes. As the government assumes additional responsibilities, such as defense, transportation, infrastructure, education, housing, food inspection, funding basic research, immigration controls, promoting the arts, it requires additional tax revenue. Once a consensus is reached as to what services the government should offer, a well-run government should impose enough taxes to fund those services. Only by fully funding the services with current taxes will the population be able to make an informed cost-benefit analysis and determine if the services are worth the expense.

The form those taxes should take (pro-rata, property, capital gains, poll, excise, import tariffs, use, consumption, income, estate, sales, wealth, licensing, payroll) is another issue. Ideally, taxes should both raise revenue and accomplish some other goal, such as encouraging conservation, protecting domestic manufacturers, or encouraging private investment, Regardless of the form of taxation, each successive increase in rates results in the government receiving less incremental revenue. Tax rates follow the law of diminishing returns.

As a simple example, a town's water tax brought in $1 million per year. The town council needs to raise $100K and so they raised the water rates by 10%—expecting to receive an additional $100K. Any economist could tell the council its approach will fail and the tax increase will probably only raise an additional $20K to $25K for the town. As the tax rate goes up, people will elect to use less water by taking shorter showers, waiting until the dishwasher is full before they run it, watering the lawn less, and so forth. This leaves an $80K hole. If, on the other hand, the council's goal had been to raise a small amount of revenue and encourage necessary water conservation because the town's aquifer is low, the rate increase would be a great success.

As taxes go, income taxes are probably the worst form of taxation. They punish hard work, risk taking, and success—traits the government should be rewarding. Income taxes also are sharply exposed to the law of diminishing returns. When income tax rates are raised:

- Some people will stop working, if working additional hours will throw them into a higher tax bracket or result in them losing an income tax credit or other subsidy.
- Some people will either retire or work fewer hours after deciding that the additional after-tax income isn't worth the extra effort required to obtain it.
- Some people will turn to tax avoidance investment strategies.
- Some people will turn to outright tax fraud.
- More people will use barter and "working off the books" to avoid reportable income.
- Many people will reduce their consumer spending on new cars, clothes, entertainment, and other nonessentials.

In any case, the economy will slow, workers will make less and pay less in taxes, perhaps resulting in a net decline in tax revenue to the government.

The bottom line is that 5% higher rates will not result in 5% higher tax revenues and might, in fact, result in a revenue decline.

CUTTING GOVERNMENT SPENDING

The size of the federal government has grown explosively over the last decade.

- In fiscal year 2001, the government spent $1.86 trillion. By fiscal year 2011, just 10 years later, the budget had exploded by more than 100% to $3.82 trillion.

- In fiscal year 2001, the number of nonmilitary employees was 1.95 million. In fiscal year 2011, that number had exploded to 2.79 million, an increase of over 80%.

In addition to the number of employees directly employed by the federal government, the number of rules and regulations created by the Federal Government has increased, meaning the private sector will be burdened by having to hire more people to interpret and comply with them. This increase in indirect mandatory hiring is unrelenting and is not dependent upon the party in control.

The United States government will have to cut spending. Spending on government has been growing at a faster rate than the economy. The ratio of government employees to workers in the private sector continues to increase. Since all wealth comes from the private sector, the public sector needs to be educated that their pay flows from the private sector. They need to support and encourage the private sector, not stifle it.

To illustrate how hard it is to cut spending, the president and Congress agreed to form a Super Committee. The committee was made up of senior senators from both parties whose seats were secure so they could propose real changes without risking their political careers. After months of work, they proposed a few modest spending reductions which, if fully enacted, would have had no significant impact at all on the debt. Their recommendations were designed to be simple, sensible ideas that both sides could rally around just to get the ball started.

Despite the trivial nature of the cuts, they were resoundingly rejected by both sides. This is the result of gerrymandering. When congressional district boundaries are drawn, they are drawn to create districts that are as "red" or "blue" as possible, so that congressmen have secure seats. That also means, however, that the congressmen have no flexibility to vote against their districts without risking their seats in Congress. If 70% of your district is conservative, you can't vote for tax increases. If 70% are liberals, the congressmen have no flexibility to reduce spending.

Figure 5.1 takes the United States' current fiscal position and translates it into equivalent numbers for a household to illustrate the trivial nature of the proposed cuts.

FIGURE 5.1

US Debt in Household Budget Terms

US Tax Revenue	$2,170,000		Family Income	$21,700
Federal Budget	$3,820,000		Family Spent	$38,200
New Debt	$1,650,000	⟹	Add'l Family Debt	$16,500
National Debt	$14,271,000		Total Family Debt	$142,710
Budget Cut	$38,500		Budget Cut	$385

Source: US Budget Office

ASSET SALES

The United States may have one way out of this financial debacle. Remarkable energy reserves in the form of natural gas under the Appalachian Mountains were recently reevaluated. This deposit, in a formation called the Marcellus Shale, runs from West Virginia across much of Pennsylvania and up through the western half of New York State. Until now, the United States' biggest natural gas field was the Barnett Shale, which covers about 20 counties in Texas. The Marcellus Shale dwarfs it both in size and in production potential. Add to this a huge oil strike in Colorado, the Arctic National Wildlife Refuge (ANWR) reserves in Alaska, and the potential to refine and export the vast quantities of oil from Canada's oil sands, and the United States has the potential to be a huge energy exporter within 10 years.

The Texas shore could have liquid propane export facilities. (It already has import facilities.) The Marcellus Shale could power the Northeast. The ANWR reserves could be exported to China. It would take a massive concerted effort between the energy industry and the federal government—bordering on our effort to put a man on the moon or to rebuild Germany and Japan—but it would be worth it. Some estimate that this would create 400,000 high-paid jobs in the energy industry plus 300,000 spin-off jobs. China could use its surplus dollars to buy the energy—solving their energy problem and our balance of trade problem. However, given the high level of animosity between the Obama administration and the fossil fuel industry, I suspect that this opportunity will be missed.

Looking at raising taxes, cutting spending, printing money, and asset sales, the odds are that the United States will take the path of least resistance and try to print its way out of this mess. By doing so, a complete global economic collapse will follow—that is, unless the United States gets beaten to it!

CHAPTER SIX

The Rest of the World

EUROPE

The only good news about the United States' current financial situation is that it is worse elsewhere. As in the United States, the European crisis built up quietly, over years, as country after country jumped on the government-induced country death spiral. By far, the worst offender was Greece. When Greece joined the European Union (EU), its government swore that its fiscal house was in order—it wasn't. For example, the Greek government left the cost of its defense department out of the budget it provided the EU. (The Greek government later claimed the size of its defense department was a secret it had to hide from Turkey.) The government also hid loans by keeping them off its balance sheet and by disguising them as swaps.

Tax fraud, bribery, and false accounting were rampant—starting at the local government level and compounding and escalating at each level of government. Finally, the lies got too big to hide, and Prime Minister Papandreou, to his credit, came clean about the deceptions of previous Greek administrations. It became immediately obvious to all its creditors that Greece would be unable to service its debt. This started a debate within the EU, and indeed within the entire western world. Was it was better to let Greece default and throw it out of the EU or to try to rescue the government?

A decision to rescue the government was made when it became clear that a complete Greek default could cause Portugal, Spain, Italy, and probably even France to default, as well. These countries' banks and pension plans owned huge amounts of both Greek debt and each other's debt. To avoid having the dominos fall, a series of bailouts were put into place. The maturity of some of Greece's debt was extended. Bond holders—primarily banks—had their arms twisted to "voluntarily" agree to accept $0.30 on the dollar just to avoid triggering the credit default swap contracts that protected against default. The banks were then provided with emergency liquidity to offset the decline in value of the Greek debt held by their governments. The banks then used that emergency liquidity money to buy more sovereign debt. If these sound like sham transactions—you're right!

In exchange for the relief, the Greek government was required to do the following:

- Raise numerous taxes and fees and put in place a system to actually collect them
- Dramatically cut spending, including government pensions and wages
- Sell assets including a casino, some Greek islands, airports, and other infrastructure

It remains to be seen which was worse, the disease or the cure. In this case, these austerity remedies caused:

- A steadily shrinking GDP
- High unemployment (22% overall, with unemployment among the young exceeding 50%)
- Massive and sometimes violent demonstrations
- Resentment by both the relatively rich countries in the north of Europe and the relatively poor countries in the south

Recently, the Greek government repurchased some its debt at about 30% of face value. Throughout the crises, the Greek people have been their own worst enemy. When the extent of the revenue shortage first became apparent, and the Greeks were informed that they were going to have to accept cuts in pay, pensions, and services, the first people to go on strike were the tax collectors. The street protests have scared away tourists—when tourism is currently Greece's most important industry.

So far, Greece has failed to meet almost all of the promises it made to secure the bailout:

- Its asset sales are way behind schedule.
- Only 440 of the more than 1,000 audits of the wealthy promised for completion by year-end 2012 have been accomplished.
- The deadline for lowering the annual deficit to 3% has been renegotiated and that deadline has been extended by 18 months.

The final chapter on Greece hasn't been written, but it appears that Greece will eventually have to leave the EU. Its economy simply keeps shrinking.

Shortly after Greece came Portugal, which needed a bailout when its economy collapsed. Soon after, Spain experienced a huge real estate bubble burst which caused its economy to stagnate. It is expected to seek a bailout. Cyprus has collapsed, and all eyes are on Italy's very weak economy; it has yet to service the world's third largest sovereign debt.

The northern European countries, including Denmark, Norway, and Germany, simply don't have enough money to bail out all of southern Europe. The future of the EU and the continued use of the Euro as a currency are both highly questionable. Given this uncertainty, it is certainly understandable that gold sales in Europe have soared over the past 10 years.

Recently, Germany asked that its approximately 3,400 tons of its gold be returned from the United States, the United Kingdom, and France, where it has been stored for the last 70+ years. Some in Germany began to question whether the United States was holding Germany's gold in an unencumbered way—that is, with no loans or swaps against it. The United States has agreed to return Germany's 1,536 tons of gold to it over the next 5 years.

THE MIDDLE EAST

Dubai surprised the world by defaulting on its debt in 2009. Excessive spending on grandiose projects like the Palm Islands and CityCenter in Las Vegas ran the emirate into financial ruin. Fortunately, a partial bailout by neighboring city-state Abu Dhabi somewhat eased the creditors' pain. Then, in December of 2010, a Tunisian fruit merchant who was tired of being extorted by the police set himself on fire. The storm of political discontent that ensued spread across the Middle East in 2011 and resulted in the overthrow and execution of Libya's dictator Muammar al-Gaddafi, the overthrow of Egypt's dictator Mubarak, and to the ongoing civil war in Syria to overthrow the dictator Bashar al-Assad. It seemed that the populations across of the entire Middle East decided to rise up against the dictators who controlled their lives.

This was colorfully referred to by the press as the "Arab Spring" and suggested that the Middle East was about to experience growth and rejuvenation. One resident of Cairo, Egypt, lamented that the skyline of the city had not changed since he was a boy. An unchanging skyline is a clear symptom of a stalled society.

Overthrowing tyrannical governments is easy. Replacing them with acceptable, functional governments is hard—especially in the Middle East. Each country has factions ranging from groups that want a Western-style secular government to Muslim extremists who want a society based entirely on Islamic law. The two do not coexist well. For these groups to form a workable government that lasts is a long shot at best. As of this writing, Egypt's new President Morsi was being thrown out of office for declaring that the interim constitutional declaration that granted him far-reaching powers shall not be subject to review by the country's supreme court. He did this to increase the power of the Muslim Brotherhood within the new government. This caused people by the tens of thousands to pour into the streets to protest the new government that was brought in power by these same protesters six months earlier—and forced him to back off. However, these actions exposed his intent and loyalties were made clear.

Likewise, the factions that are fighting Assad in Syria are already arguing among themselves about what the post-Assad government will look like, despite the fact that they haven't yet won the war against Assad.

The problem with the Arab Spring was that it raised the expectations of the people, particularly the young people. To date, their futures have not improved, and they are becoming restless. Basic services from water to electricity to sanitation are breaking down, as no one is in charge or can spend money or collect taxes.

The Middle East has been at war (in one form or another) for over a thousand years. It won't take much to start another war.

Additionally, the clock is clearly running out on the Israel–Iran stalemate over nuclear weapons. It would be foolish to expect peace in the Middle East in our lifetime. Finally, wars in the Middle East often draw in others and, thus, have the ability to escalate. Times of war are often the best times to hold alternative investments, because the need for those commodities soars, and the supply lines are often interrupted.

AFRICA

Throughout the nineteenth century, Africa had its problems. Some, like shaking off the last remnants of colonialism and droughts, were not of its own making. Others, like the endless civil and tribal wars, corruption, lack of respect for contracts, and lack of investment in infrastructure, were. Many African nations have completed the death cycle, recovered, and then completed the death cycle again—apparently learning nothing from the earlier collapse(s).

In the north, Mali is in a state of civil war with Islamic fundamentalists who are challenging the secular government. France has been dragged in to defend the current government, largely because France's uranium comes from Africa and France is very dependent upon nuclear power. Given the large Islamic population now living in France, this is causing problems in both Africa and France. Algeria has an Islamic terrorist problem, as the refinery attack in January of 2013 clearly illustrated. Libya is in a state of chaos as factions maneuver for control.

In the south, Zimbabwe printed so much currency that its currency became an international joke, as the $100 trillion Zimbabwe note shown in Figure 6.1 indicates. Of course, the country could proudly state that it never defaulted on its debt—if your only definition of default is "not being repaid." If you include "being repaid in worthless currency" as default, then Zimbabwe defaulted. Today, the country actually runs on US dollars, as well as silver and gold coins. Africa does have a few examples of countries that have long-term success, including South Africa, Morocco, and Madagascar.

FIGURE 6.1

$100 Trillion Zimbabwe Note

CENTRAL AND SOUTH AMERICA

Not to be left out, parts of Central and South America are also in the race to be the catalyst for the next financial catastrophe. Here are some examples:

- The Mexican government appears to have lost control of large sections of its own territory to drug cartels.
- Argentina is experiencing hyperinflation and has imposed currency controls. It is in the last stage of decline before total collapse.

- In 2007, Venezuela nationalized the oil deposits of the country and demanded companies cede a 60% stake in all oil projects in Venezuela to state-owned oil company PDVSA. ExxonMobil and ConocoPhillips walked away from their investments and sought $40 billion in damages from the Venezuelan government. In the interim, Venezuela used the oil reserves as collateral to borrow money from China. Venezuela will pay the interest in oil. Unfortunately for Venezuela, and perhaps China, a Paris-based International Chamber of Commerce arbitration panel awarded $908 million to Exxon. (Exxon wanted $10 billion.) The World Bank's International Centre for Settlement of Investment Disputes may decide to take up the case. Venezuela has already stated that even if Exxon wins damages, it will not pay them. Venezuela's economy has been so devastated by Chavez's and Maduro's policies that basic staples have disappeared from the market. Recently the country had to make emergency purchases of toilet paper, which had been unavailable for weeks.
- Ecuador is trying to extort $19 billion from Chevron for environmental damage, despite the fact that, when Chevron sold its oil operation to Ecuador, it was granted a full waiver of liability. This attempted theft has almost killed new investment in Ecuador.

JAPAN

The "award" for the major nation in the most debt relative to GDP goes to Japan. As of the end of 2012, Japan's debt stood at 233% of GDP, as shown in Figure 6.2. This is much higher than Greece's debt. However, Japan's citizens are great savers—typically saving 20% of their income. This has allowed Japan to finance itself by borrowing from its own citizens.

When Japan's export-dependent economy began to slow, Japan shifted to internal projects to stimulate the economy—primarily infrastructure projects. Japan spent trillions of yen improving its highways, bridges, ports, airports, train system, power systems, and the like. The idea was that the public investment would make the private sector more competitive on a global basis. That hasn't worked out, as Japan's economy has grown only very slowly over the past two decades.

Recently, Japan has suffered from two setbacks:

1. The Tōhoku earthquake and tsunami that hit Japan in 2011 was devastating. The total cost of the cleanup will run into the trillions of yen. The decision to shut down all of Japan's nuclear plans was an aftereffect that will raise Japan's energy costs substantially and forever.
2. The dispute with China over the Senkaku Islands (called Diaoyu Islands in China), which may or may not have oil beneath them, might require Japan to spend hundreds of trillions of yen it doesn't have on defense and/or go to war with China—a war it cannot hope to win.

Japan's new prime minister, Shinzō Abe, just announced that Japan will go on a massive money printing campaign to lower the value of the yen and make Japan's products more competitive. The first stage is a ¥10.3 trillion stimulus package for public works that hopefully will create 600,000 jobs.

FIGURE 6.2

Country Debt Loads Compared to GDP

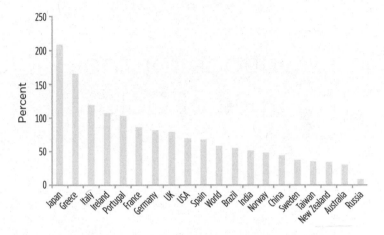

The bottom line is that around the world, fuses are burning. Some, perhaps most, will burn out before they trigger an explosion. However, some of these fuses will trigger explosions that will have global repercussions.

CHAPTER SEVEN

Outlook for the Price of Gold

Given the fiscal, monetary, and geopolitical chaos, it is little wonder precious metals have been the best performing asset class over the last decade with 11 straight years of positive appreciation. Now let's look to the future. At the end of the day, the price of any commodity is simply a function of supply and demand. Let's look first at the demand side.

Future Demand for Gold

The demand for gold comes from five sources: use in industrial applications, use in medical applications, use as a currency, use as a store of wealth, and use in the manufacture of jewelry. Of these, the first two are minor and are mentioned only for the sake of completeness:

- **Industrial Applications**—Gold has three primary industrial applications:

- *Batteries*—Adding a small amount of gold to a battery creates a super battery that can store up to ten times the power of traditional lithium batteries. While expensive, batteries that incorporate gold are used in an increasing number of mission critical applications by private corporations and governments.
- *Electronics*—Gold is frequently used to plate cable and printed circuit board connections because of its unparalleled conductive capability. It is also used for connectors and wires within semiconductors.
- *Catalytic converters*—Gold can also be used in catalytic converters instead of platinum. This makes sense when gold is cheaper than platinum. New gold compounds are being promoted as being 40% more efficient than platinum at converting the highly toxic carbon monoxide in car exhaust into harmless carbon dioxide.

- **Medicinal Applications**—Medicinal applications for gold have been known for more than 5,000 years.
  - Salts, taken orally or injected, can reduce the pain of arthritis.
  - Taken orally, an isotope of gold seems to augment the effectiveness of other cancer treatments.
  - Gold is a natural bacterial agent and, therefore, reduces the risk of infection when used with implants of any kind.
- **Currency**—In the past, almost all currency was in the form of gold or silver coins. Today, the direct use of gold as a day-to-day currency is relegated to sections of the Middle East, Asia, and Africa. However, it quickly reappears wherever paper currency has collapsed or where people simply don't trust paper currencies. It also reappears whenever privacy is an issue. For example, as of this writing, Turkey's government is buying oil from Iran despite the UN embargo on Iran

and is paying for the oil with gold. Ordinarily, the payments from Turkey to Iran would go through the Society for Worldwide Interbank Financial Telecommunication (SWIFT) payment system—but this system is closed to Iran. Gold rides to the rescue!

- **Wealth Storage**—An ever-increasing range of investors, from the largest supra-national organizations down to the poorest individuals, store a portion of their wealth in the form of gold bullion or gold coins.

Supra-national organizations transcend countries and include entities such as the United Nations, the World Bank, and the International Monetary Fund (IMF). For example, the IMF owns over 3,000 tons of gold. It can either lend this gold directly to needy nations, or can use this gold as collateral to borrow paper currencies and lend them to needy nations. What is not known outside the IMF is how much of this gold is encumbered—meaning that it is serving as collateral for loans or swaps and, therefore, not available for sale.

Governments hold substantial quantities of gold. In the fairly recent past, governments were the largest sellers of gold. For example:

- The United Kingdom sold 400 tons (more than 50% of Britain's reserves) between 1999 and 2002 when the price was at a 20-year low.
- The Swiss sold over 1,300 tons between 2000 and 2005.

Today, smart governments have realized the error of their ways and are buying gold—albeit at prices that are 50% to 600% higher than the prices at which they sold. For instance:

- The United States owns over 8,134 tons of gold, or approximately $1,000 per person; some, most, or all of that gold may be encumbered.
- Germany owns over 3,401 tons, approximately $4,500 per person.
- France owns 2,435 tons.
- China owns 1,100 tons.
- Switzerland still owns over 1,040 tons, approximately $6,000 per person.
- Russia owns 920 tons, 9.2% of their reserves.
- Japan owns 766 tons, 3% of their reserves.
- The Netherlands owns 613 tons, 60% of their reserves.
- India owns 560 tons, 10% of their reserves.

Others countries are adding gold to their reserves:

- South Korea added 14 tons.
- Brazil doubled its holdings in a year.
- Paraguay bought 7.5 tons.
- Argentina added 7 tons.
- Columbia added more than 2 tons.

While numerous countries are buying gold (Figure 7.2 shows the shift in gold holdings from western countries to eastern countries from 1950 through 2012), the big government gold stories are Russia, India, Vietnam, and China.

Russia holds a lot of its reserves in the form of US dollars. The Putin government has stated publicly that it wants to reduce its reserves of US dollars. The Russians have proposed that a basket of currencies or IMF special drawing rights replace the US dollar—with little success. In the meantime, Russia is systematically replacing its dollar reserves with gold.

India has a love-hate affair with gold. The people love it, and the government hates it. India and China are vying for the position of world's top gold importer. The people prefer gold because they don't trust the government to correctly manage the country's money supply. Inflation in India is often in the double digit range. On the other hand, the government views the money its people invest in gold as "dead money" that could be more productively employed if it was invested in the mainstream economy. Given the Indian population's long love affair with gold, the government has its work cut out.

The Indian government recently imposed an import duty to raise the price of gold and discourage its importation. Unfortunately, as is almost always the case, the duty had the opposite effect. The duty caused a rush to buy, and the people bought 30 metric tons in just five days instead of the usual 5–6 tons, as they feared even higher duties in the future. The duty also makes smuggling gold into India profitable.

Vietnam is a society on the verge of economic collapse. The country is printing money like crazy and by doing so, is causing the value of its currency (the dong) to plummet (USD80 = VND1MM). The people are trying to protect themselves by buying gold as an inflation hedge. The government, as all governments do in this situation, is trying to prohibit the importation and purchase of gold so that the people are forced to hold its paper currency— even as its value declines to zero.

China holds approximately $2 trillion worth of US Treasury securities in its reserves. It also is rapidly accumulating gold. Unlike Russia, however, it doesn't release timely reports of how much it has acquired. The Chinese government is encouraging, and financially supporting, domestic production and is buying up almost all of the production from its own mines, as shown in Figure 7.1.

Instead of buying bullion in the open market, which would push up the price, China has been buying further back in the production cycle. They are buying mines and mining rights. They are particularly active in Australia, Canada, Afghanistan, and Africa. Much of the gold imported into Hong Kong is really being bought by China. Many Western analysts expect China to announce a gold-backed renminbi that it will use to try to displace the USD as the world's reserve currency. The Chinese government also encourages its citizens to hold gold coins and bullion. Gold can be purchased at any major bank in China.

FIGURE 7.1

Chinese Gold Production and Imports

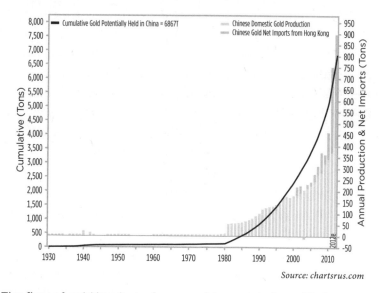

Source: chartsrus.com

The flow of gold has been from west to east, in line with the movement of wealth.

FIGURE 7.2

World Gold Reserves

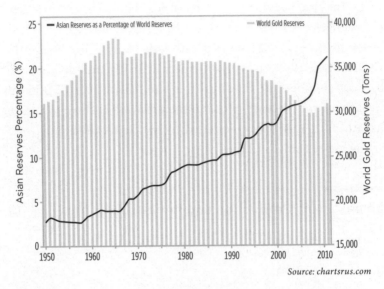

Source: *chartsrus.com*

The central banks added 536 tons of gold to their holdings in 2012—the most in more than a half century. The world seems to be moving toward a gold standard by natural selection and acclamation.

US Institutions and Companies

Entities such as banks, insurance companies, and pension plans currently hold almost no gold. That, however, is changing! US banks can now hold gold as tier one capital—meaning that gold is considered to be the equivalent of cash in the vault. While physical cash offers no return, gold can offer a return, and banks are expected to add gold to their capital structure. Pension plans are now permitted to buy gold as a natural hedge for their paper (stocks and bonds) investments. The University of Texas Investment Management Company, which manages the pension plan for the University of Texas, recently bought $500 million in gold. Insurance

FIGURE 7.3

World Gold Holdings

		Tons	% of reserves				Tons	% of reserves
1	United States	8,133.5	77%		21	Austria	280.0	57%
2	Germany	3,395.5	74%		22	Belgium	227.5	41%
3	IMF	2,814.0	-		23	Philippines	193.4	13%
4	Italy	2,451.8	73%		24	Algeria	173.6	5%
5	France	2,435.4	73%		25	Thailand	152.4	5%
6	China	1,054.1	2%		26	Singapore	127.4	3%
7	Switzerland	1,040.1	12%		27	Sweden	125.7	14%
8	Russia	934.5	10%		28	South Africa	125.0	14%
9	Japan	765.2	3%		29	Mexico	125.0	4%
10	The Netherlands	612.5	61%		30	Libya	116.6	6%
11	India	557.7	11%		31	BIS	116.0	-
12	ECB	502.1	34%		32	Greece	111.8	83%
13	Taiwan	423.6	6%		33	Kazakhstan	104.0	20%
14	Portugal	382.5	91%		34	Romania	103.7	12%
15	Venezuela	362.0	74%		35	Poland	102.9	6%
16	Saudi Arabia	322.9	3%		36	Australia	79.9	10%
17	United Kingdom	310.3	17%		37	Kuwait	79.0	14%
18	Turkey	302.4	15%		38	Egypt	75.6	26%
19	Lebanon	286.8	31%		39	Indonesia	73.1	4%
20	Spain	281.6	31%		40	Korea	70.4	1%

Source: IMF, World Gold Council

companies also can buy gold. Northwestern Mutual Life recently bought $400 million in gold. If even a small percentage of US banks, pension plans, and insurance companies were each to put a small percentage of their portfolios into gold, the additional demand would cause a significant price increase.

Hedge Funds and Money Managers

Hedge funds and money managers have always been active in the commodity markets. Some of the largest and most successful hedge fund managers hold substantial portfolios of gold. In some cases, the gold is held in physical form—bullion bars at a depository. Other hedge funds/managers just have large positions in GLD or other exchange traded funds. (See Figure 7.4 for the holders of the largest positions of this writing.)

FIGURE 7.4

Largest Holders of GLD

Holder Name	Portfolio Name	Source	Opt	Amt Held	% Out	Latest Chg	File Dt
		All Sources	All				
1 PAULSON & CO	PAULSON & CO	13F		21,837,552	4.95	0	09/30/12
2 NORTHERN TRUST CORPORATION	NORTHERN TRUST CORPO	13F		16,976,028	3.85	353,084	09/30/12
3 BLACKROCK	n/a	ULT-AGG	Y	9,177,149	2.08	2,538,424	09/30/12
4 BANK OF AMERICA CORPORATION	BANK OF AMERICA	ULT-AGG	Y	8,883,698	2.01	120,424	09/30/12
5 JPMORGAN CHASE & CO	n/a	ULT-AGG	Y	7,462,211	1.69	-413,837	09/30/12
6 MORGAN STANLEY	n/a	ULT-AGG		6,472,599	1.47	18,544	09/30/12
7 ALLIANZ ASSET MANAGEMENT A	n/a	ULT-AGG		6,224,454	1.41	-94,319	09/30/12
8 CREDIT SUISSE AG	CREDIT SUISSE AG	13F	Y	6,029,808	1.37	-1,181,882	09/30/12
9 FMR LLC	n/a	ULT-AGG		4,670,287	1.06	1,389,920	09/30/12
10 UBS	n/a	ULT-AGG	Y	3,430,508	0.78	-2,003,660	09/30/12
11 CI INVESTMENTS INC	CI INVESTMENTS INC	13F		3,387,836	0.77	1,793,293	12/31/12
12 GOLDMAN SACHS GROUP INC	GOLDMAN SACHS GROUP I	13F	Y	2,688,776	0.61	912,241	09/30/12
13 LONE PINE CAPITAL LLC	LONE PINE CAPITAL LLC	13F		2,587,216	0.59	-1,163,132	09/30/12
14 DEUTSCHE BANK AG	DEUTSCHE BANK AKTIENG	13F	Y	2,488,084	0.56	1,141,243	09/30/12
15 FIRST EAGLE INVESTMENT MGM	FIRST EAGLE INVESTMENT	13F		2,483,660	0.56	-752,636	09/30/12
16 LAZARD ASSET MANAGEMENT	n/a	ULT-AGG		2,421,323	0.55	-4,995	12/31/12
17 LAURION CAPITAL MANAGEMENT	LAURION CAPITAL MANAG	13F	Y	2,327,642	0.53	78,795	09/30/12
18 TD ASSET MANAGEMENT INC	TD ASSET MANAGEMENT IN	13F		2,181,060	0.49	244,447	09/30/12

Source: Bloomberg

Individuals

Perhaps the biggest variable in the demand for gold is the demand by individuals who increasingly are buying gold as a hedge against paper currency. Precise numbers are hard to get, because most gold buyers are very quiet about their purchases. Individuals buy gold when the real return from traditional investments is negative. In the United States, this is defined as the yield on T-bills minus inflation. When investors lose buying power by holding T-bills, they look for alternative investments, as shown in Figure 7.5.

FIGURE 7.5

Gold vs. Real Interest Rates

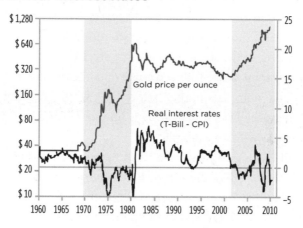

FACTORS IMPACTING SUPPLY

Mining gold adds new gold to the world's supply. Figure 7.6 shows the approximate number of tons of gold produced each year from 2006 through 2012, according to the World Gold Council.

FIGURE 7.6

Tons Produced

Year	Tons Produced
2006	2360
2007	2340
2008	2280
2009	2390
2010	2440
2011	2480
2012	2510

The World Gold Council's figures are only estimates, however, since gold is mined illegally by small (and not so small) mining operations that often trespass on property where they have no mining rights. (The trials and travails of mining are discussed later in this chapter in the section on mining stocks.)

Not all of those tons produced come onto the market. Some tons of gold came onto the market before they were taken out of the ground because of the way mining is financed. The best way to illustrate this is with an example.

A small mining company wants to borrow $50 million from a bank. The bank offers the mine three repayment alternatives, as shown in Figure 7.7. For the sake of simplicity, let's assume annual interest payments at the end of the year.

- **Alternative A**—Under this option, the mine pays 10% interest on the outstanding principal. In the first 5 years, the mine makes interest-only payments, followed by 5 years of repaying $10 million of principal plus interest. After 10 years, the remaining principal is repaid.

- **Alternative B**—This option utilizes the same payment schedule as Alternative A—but to be paid in gold. Assuming the parties fix the price of gold at $2,000 an ounce—regardless of its true current market value—then, in the first 5 years, the mine pays the bank 2,500 ounces. In years 6–10, the mine pays 7,500, 7,000, 6,500, 6,000, and 5,500 ounces respectively.

- **Alternative C**—Under this option, the mine pays 50% of the gold the mine produces—whether the mine produces 1 ounce or 1 million ounces.

FIGURE 7.7

Three Alternatives Assuming $2,000 and $50 Million

Alt	Year 1	Year 2	Year 3	Year 4	Year 5	Year 6	Year 7	Year 8	Year 9	Year 10
A	$5MM	$5MM	$5MM	$5MM	$5MM	$15MM	$14MM	$13MM	$12MM	$11MM
B	2,500 oz.	2,500 oz.	2,500 oz.	2,500 oz.	2,500 oz.	7,500 oz.	7,500 oz.	6,500 oz.	6,000 oz.	5,500 oz.
C	50%	50%	50%	50%	50%	50%	50%	50%	50%	50%

Which of these is the best alternative for the mining company, naturally, depends upon how successful the mine is and what happens to the price of gold. If the mine is a huge success, and the price of gold soars, then paying the interest in fixed dollars is the cheapest financing. However, if the mine is weak and the price of gold falls, the mine would rather give the bank half of its meager output because that will cost much less than the $50 million it originally borrowed.

If the miner and bank elect choice B or C, the bank will be "long gold." This means that the bank will receive gold in the future and hopes its value will rise. Under alternative B, the bank expects to receive 45,000 ounces. Under alternative C, the bank hopes to receive even more. The bank can simply assume the price risk of receiving gold in the future and book profits (if the price of gold rises) or losses (if the price of gold declines). Alternatively, the bank could hedge this risk by borrowing 45,000 ounces of gold from other investors who already own it. Owners lend gold to a bank because lending relieves them of the responsibility of paying storage and insurance charges. Depending upon the level of demand, the owners may also receive a small fee from the bank for lending their gold. Usually, the investors who lend gold to a bank can demand its return at any time. The bank then sells the gold it just borrowed in the open market in order to receive the cash required to make this $50 million loan and other loans, as well (45,000 ounces × $2,000 ounce = $90,000,000).

As the bank receives gold from the mining company, it uses that gold to repay the investors that lent them gold. Thus, it's the signing of the mine financing agreement that causes 45,000 ounces of gold to be sold—not the mining of the 45,000 ounces. As the gold is actually mined, it doesn't come to the market, it goes to the party that loaned the gold to the bank. Figure 7.8 and Figure 7.9 provide visual representations of the transactions.

FIGURE 7.8

Mine Financing—Origination

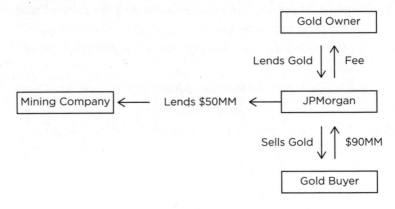

FIGURE 7.9

Mine Financing—Term of Loan

Scrap

In addition to newly mined gold, the other major source of gold is recycled scrap gold. Most of the gold mined throughout history is still with us; it is too valuable to lose. While some small jewelry pieces are undoubtedly lost and more than one miser has gone to his death without disclosing where his secret cache of gold is buried, the vast majority of gold is recycled and reused. The gold in a US wedding ring might have been in the necklace of an Athenian merchant, then of a Chinese warlord, then in the bracelet of a Spanish noble, and the ring of a US pirate.

Every pawnshop and most jewelers will buy gold for scrap value. A combination of high gold prices and tough economic times increases the amount of scrap that is sold. When, in 2011, the price of gold soared above $1,900 per ounce, the scrap market soared as people sold broken chains, orphaned earrings, out-of-style jewelry, or jewelry that was rarely worn. For those individuals who lost jobs, gold was sold to make a car or mortgage payments. The scrap business was at its highest in Greece due to Greece's economic collapse. The scrap business can add 200–300 tons a year to supply.

Recovery

A fairly minor source of gold today—but one that is growing rapidly—is the recovery of gold from broken or obsolete electronics. Almost every cell phone, game machine, television, computer, tablet, and so on, has some gold in it. A ton of electronic waste contains 8–16 ounces of gold, a much higher concentration than most gold-bearing rock. Historically, recovery required someone to disassemble the electronics. Then, the gold was leached from the CPU and other high gold components using mercury and/or cyanide. Done this way, the recovery business is both extremely environmentally unfriendly and dangerous, if not deadly, for the workers. Currently, almost all the recovery work in China is done this way. There, environmental protection and worker safety rules are nonexistent or simply ignored.

A more modern approach grinds and chops electronics, just the way that gold-bearing rock is ground. The gold is then extracted using traditional techniques. Given the incredible volume of obsolete electronics available for recycling, there are numerous start-up companies developing processes to recover gold from electronics on a large scale. Someday, when the process is perfected, this may add 400 tons a year to the supply.

CHAPTER EIGHT

Arguments Against Gold

Now, let's look at the arguments against gold as a good investment and the oft-cited answers to those arguments:

- Gold is only a yellow rock and has limited practical utility, or so the argument goes. Why hold $100 million in gold, when for the same $100 million you can own a specialty steel manufacturing plant? The rock can't do anything but "look pretty." A steel plant can produce a very useful product—steel. The plant has better utility in that it can generate a return. This argument however is moot since the choice is not an either/or. No one is suggesting an investor own only gold, but only that it makes sense to own some gold to provide purchasing power when there is no demand for steel or in the event that the plant suffers a catastrophic loss. Also, the plant can't be easily moved—gold can.
- Gold doesn't generate current income. That's true, but then, neither does a growth stock, a zero coupon bond, or a piece

of artwork. Gold doesn't generate income because it doesn't have to in order to provide a positive real return. It appreciates in currency terms. CDs and T-bills have to offer interest because the buying power of the dollar declines, and no one would hold them if they didn't pay interest as compensation for this decline. In fact, since the Fed came into existence with a mandate to protect the purchasing power of the dollar, the actual purchasing power has dropped by 98%. Figure 8.1 shows the decline in purchasing power from 1920 through 2009. Clearly the Fed has failed miserably in its mission to defend the dollar. The Fed is not alone in this failure. As Figure 8.2 indicates, every major fiat currency has plunged relative to gold.

FIGURE 8.1

Value of the Dollar

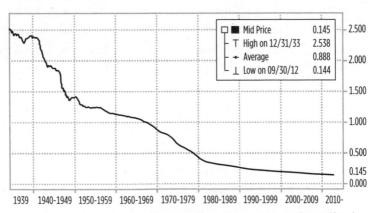

☐ ■ Mid Price	0.145		2.500
T High on 12/31/33	2.538		
⬩ Average	0.888		2.000
⊥ Low on 09/30/12	0.144		

Source: Bloomberg

FIGURE 8.2

Currencies vs. Gold

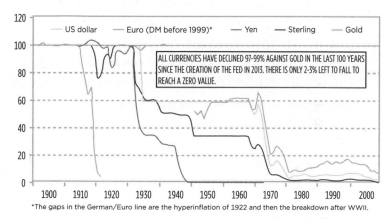

*The gaps in the German/Euro line are the hyperinflation of 1922 and then the breakdown after WWII.

Source: World Gold Council

- Gold is subject to adverse tax treatment. In the United States, physical gold is taxed as a collectible. As of this writing the tax rate on collectibles is higher (28%) than the capital gains rate on stocks and bonds (0% to 23.8%). Higher tax rates are always a negative.

- Gold is a barbaric relic. Many economists regard gold as a barbaric relic. While it is true that many economists think gold's days are over, most of them are Keynesians, who believe in the economic theories put forth by John Keynes. Keynes believed that to minimize the business cycle, the Fed should increase the money supply when the country is in a recession and decrease it when in an expansion. Other economists, those belonging to the Austrian School of Economics, would disagree and still regard gold as a nearly perfect currency. While some economists argue that gold is a relic, the other five billion people who live on this planet still desire to own it. It is best to side with the overwhelming majority. Besides, the Keynesian economists have nothing useful to offer in lieu of gold except fiat currencies. Throughout history, every fiat currency has eventually failed.

- Gold underperforms when compared with stocks. This is a silly argument. Whether gold or stocks outperform depends on which stocks you own—and over what time frame you measure performance. A portfolio of Apple, Microsoft, Oracle, Walmart, and similar stocks outperforms gold. Gold outperformed a portfolio of Enron, WorldCom, Parmalat, HealthSouth, and the like. Even if you compare the performance of gold to the S&P 500 index, the time period you look at will distort the result. It is clear however from historical evidence that the price of gold can reach a multiple of the value for the S&P 500:

  - In the 1930s, the price of gold reached 4.5 times the value of the S&P 500.
  - In the 1970s, the price of gold reached 2.7 times the value of the S&P 500.
  - In the 1990s, the price of gold reached almost 6 times the value of the S&P 500.
  - As of this writing, the price of gold is just over 1 times value of the S&P 500.

- Gold deflates prices. A gold standard results in price deflation as productivity increases outpace the increase in the supply of money. This may be true. The net effect of monetary deflation is that savers are rewarded at the expense of debtors. Money becomes more valuable while sitting in a desk drawer. Why is this worse than the system we have now, where inflation rewards debtors and brutally punishes savers?

- Gold is too expensive. Actually, despite the recent rise in price, on a relative basis gold is historically quite inexpensive—consider the following:
  - In 1935, when an ounce of gold was worth $35:
    - A quality suit cost $19.75—or 0.56 ounces of gold.
    - A family car cost $500—or 14.3 ounces of gold.
    - The average price of a house was $7,150—or 204.2 ounces of gold.
  - As of this writing, with gold at $1,800 an ounce:
    - A quality suit costs $600—or 0.3 ounces of gold.
    - A family car now costs $18,160—or 10 ounces of gold.
    - The price of a house averages $181,100—or 101 ounces of gold. (Admittedly, housing prices are temporarily depressed.)
  - Based upon data from the US Social Security Administration, the wages of an average earner with an income of $8,031 could be used to purchase 10 ounces of gold. In 2012, that average income had increased to $42,500 and could purchase 23 ounces of gold.
  - In 1971, 180 ounces of gold were required to buy a Cadillac Eldorado. In 2012, 90 ounces would buy a Cadillac XLR.

As indicated in Figure 8.3, gold may still have a significant upside.

FIGURE 8.3

Historic Bull Market

Underlying Instruments	Dates	Increase in Value
Gold	1970s	2,000%
Nasdaq	1990s	1,250%
S&P 500	1982–2000	1,250%
Bond Prices	1980–2000	1,200%
Crude Oil	1990–2008	900%
Dow Transports	1980–1990	500%
Japan Land	1980s	500%
Nikkei	1980s	500%
Gold	2000—?	500%

CHAPTER NINE

Alternative Ways to Buy Gold

There are ten alternative ways for individuals to gain exposure to gold:

- Buy physical gold outright
- Buy physical gold on margin
- Buy forward contracts
- Buy futures contracts
- Buy ETFs
- Buy ELNs
- Buy mining stocks
- Invest in royalty trusts
- Buy gold in the ground
- Buy jewelry

Naturally, each alternative has its own advantages and disadvantages.

Buy Physical Gold Outright

The first way to own gold is to simply buy gold coins or bullion and take delivery:

- Unlike buying bonds, CDs, T-bills, or any other debt instrument where your asset is someone else's liability, possessing physical gold frees you from worrying about whether any counterparty will perform. When you own gold, no one has to pay you interest, return your principal, etc.
- Unlike buying a gold certificate or ETF, you don't have to worry about whether the fund has enough metal to back all its shares. You don't have to worry about the government indirectly seizing your gold by seizing the fund's gold.
- When you possess physical gold, you always have access to it when you need it—provided you keep it nearby.

The major disadvantage of owning physical gold is that gold is fungible; if your gold is lost or stolen, there is no way to identify it. Therefore, it must be protected. To protect it, you must store it safely:

- Hide it carefully either above or below ground—but that's no guarantee that someone won't find it. There is all sorts of advice available on how best to hide gold. For example, if you bury it outside, you want it at least 4 feet deep—well below the range of most metal detectors. Many apartment dwellers choose to open a hole on a wall near the floor, place the gold inside the wall, and then spackle and paint.
- Store it in a safe deposit box at a bank or private storage facility. A private facility is preferable; they are less regulated.

There's a private depository in Las Vegas that identifies you with a retina scan and collects no other information about you. To gain access to your box, they scan your eye and you enter a password. You have the only keys to your box. No subpoena from any court will violate your privacy or allow another party entry to your box because the company has no way of identifying that it's your box.

- Store it in a home safe. Be careful here, because a home safe proves no protection if a thief steals the entire safe, holds a gun to your head, or holds a gun to a member of your family's head. Some store their gold in several locations for just this scenario.
- Store it in another country. This places your gold outside the legal jurisdiction of your home country and helps protect against confiscation.

You will have to decide whether to insure your gold. Insuring gold coins is expensive (1% to 3% per year) and requires you to disclose your holdings, which are then kept in a "confidential" file at the insurance company.

Perhaps the most popular way to buy precious metals is via the 1 troy ounce coins. The coins shown in Figure 9.1 all contain 1 troy ounce of metal. The Vienna Philharmonic and the American Buffalo are 99.9999% pure gold and weigh 1 ounce. The others range from 99.9% to 99.99% pure and weigh more than an ounce, as other metals are added to strengthen the coins.

FIGURE 9.1

Common Precious Metal Coins

In addition to 1-ounce coins, gold coins also come in half-ounce, quarter-ounce, and 1/10-ounce sizes. Note that the markup is usually a little higher on the smaller coins since they are less liquid.

Pawn shops and neighborhood coin shops will sell to you or buy 1 to 10 coins from you. Small quantities also can be bought and sold via eBay and other internet sites. Serious investors who want 10 to upwards of 1,000 coins turn to a trusted dealer. Choosing a dealer to use is a critical decision. It seems every other week there's a story about a gold dealer who goes bankrupt and causes customer losses. Investors should look for a dealer with the following characteristics:

- **Integrity**—The integrity of the company's management and sales advisors must be beyond reproach. This is sometimes hard to determine. The gold coin business attracts its share of charlatans and quick-buck artists. Beware of companies that have to use celebrity endorsements to gain the air of respectability. These celebrity endorsements are very expensive, and it's the investors who ultimately pay their fees.

- **Exclusivity**—Does the company have the right to buy directly from the United States' and Canadian mints? If not, the company has to buy from a company that can buy from the mints, and that adds a second markup onto the cost of the coins. Figure 9.2 shows a Red Box, the 500 gold coin box from the US Mint.

- **Longevity**—The longer the company has been in business, the better. It is preferable if the company is multigenerational.

- **Inventory**—The US Mint, the Royal Canadian Mint, and other coin producers periodically run short of coins, so it is important your dealer maintains a significant inventory so you can buy the coins you want without incurring long delays until delivery.

- **Liquidity**—While investors start off by buying, at some point, they will want to sell. You want a dealer that guarantees to repurchase everything they sold you at a fair bid price.

- **Transparency**—The dealer should have a web site where buyers can see the current price of the various investment alternatives and the pricing policies for both buyers and sellers.

- **Information**—The dealer should be able to provide you with background information, research, and historic data on the various metals and coins.

- **Service**—The company should offer toll-free numbers and have long office hours. Your account executive should have a backup so that, when he or she is away or unavailable, someone who is familiar with your account and your objectives can help you.

Author's personal note: I have used numerous dealers over the years (and have the scars to prove it). I am pleased to recommend Mark Patton at Monex Inc. (Monex.com). If you have a serious interest in acquiring physical metal, give him a call at (800) 949-4653, ext. 2294.

FIGURE 9.2

The Red Box—US 500 Gold Coin Box from the US Mint

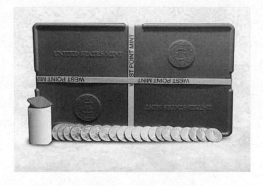

In addition to selling coins, dealers also sell bullion bars, in sizes from 1/10 of an ounce up to 1,000 ounces. The most liquid bars are created by the world's most respected fabricators, including Engelhard, PAMP Suisse, Credit Suisse, the Perth Mint, and Johnson Matthey. Larger bars are typically stamped with a unique bar number and weight. The older the bar, the less accurate the weight on the bar will be. One hundred years ago, people poured molten gold into rough molds, so the bars are not exactly the size stated on the bar. New bars are created in facilities that have the technology to pour precisely weighted bars. Today, when investors buy or sell old or new bars, they are weighed to within 1/1,000 of an ounce for pricing purposes.

LEVERAGED GOLD

In a leveraged gold transaction, investors put up a down payment of 10% or more of the gold's value and borrow the balance of the purchase price, so they can buy more gold than they could if they paid cash. If the price of gold goes up faster than the after-tax interest expense, the leverage increases the investor's annualized return. For the dealer's and the investor's protection, the gold should be stored at an independent third party depository, in the investor's name, until the gold is sold or the loan is retired. Once the loan is paid off, the gold can either be delivered to the investor or the investor can continue to store it in segregated safekeeping. In the United States, the only firm with both decades of experience and an unblemished record in offering investors the ability to buy physical gold on margin is Monex, Inc. (monex.com) via their Atlas Program.

FORWARD CONTRACTS

A forward contract is a contract between a dealer and investor in which an investor agrees to buy and the dealer agrees to sell a certain quantity of gold at a certain price—but the actual transaction doesn't occur until some point in the future. The price the investor pays will be approximately the spot price on the day the parties enter the transaction plus the dealer's cost of storing the gold until it is delivered. The advantages of this approach are that the contract can be very flexible. It can be for any quantity of gold in any form (coins, bullion). The contracts also frequently allow the investor to leverage the investment by only requiring a 10% to 20% down payment. The downside includes:

- **Counterparty risk**—Either party maybe unwilling or unable to honor its commitment when the contract comes due.
- **Limited liquidity**—Since this a private contract, the only way out is to renegotiate the deal with the counterparty.

For a complete discussion of forwards, see my book *The Investor's Guidebook to Derivatives.*

FUTURES CONTRACTS

A futures contract is a publicly traded forward contract. The advantage is that the exchange guarantees all trades—virtually eliminating counterparty risk. It also has excellent liquidity. The disadvantage is that the contract limits the flexibility of the investment to certain sizes (100 ounces and multiples thereof) and to certain delivery dates. Arbitrage theory suggests that futures contracts should be priced at spot plus the cost of carry. Since it always costs money to store gold, the future price should always be higher. For example, if it costs $50 to store an ounce of gold for a year and the spot price today is $2,000, it doesn't matter whether you buy it for $2,000 today and pay $50 to store it or agree to buy it in a year $2,050. Likewise, it doesn't matter if you buy it today for $2,000 and pay $100 to store it for two years or simply agree to buy the gold in two years for $2,100.

While the pricing theory is straightforward, there are a variety of technical and market factors which can distort the future price. These factors can cause issues with ETFs that fund with futures, as shown in Figure 9.3.

FIGURE 9.3

Expected Future Prices of Gold Futures

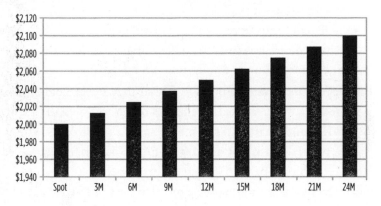

EXCHANGE TRADED FUNDS (ETFs)

Gold ETFs are mutual funds that only invest in gold. Shares in the trust represent undivided interests in the fund's trust account. The money the fund raises from selling shares is used to buy gold and pay the storage fees and the fund's operating expenses.

The advantages of ETFs include:

- Buying and selling ETF shares incurs lower transaction costs than buying the physical metal. ETF transactions cost investors the same brokerage commissions as other listed stocks; typically $8.00 to $15.00 for up to 5,000 shares. This makes ETFs very attractive for short-term trades.
- Gold held by ETFs has lower per-ounce storage and insurance expenses than gold held by individual investors. Large vault rooms are less expensive per cubic foot than retail safe deposit boxes.

- ETF shares are amazingly liquid. Investors can buy, sell, or short gold in size without impacting the market anytime the market is open.
- Different funds store their gold in different parts of the world, which allows investors to hedge storage location risk.

The biggest disadvantage of ETFs is that they never hold enough metal to back every share. If the fund's directors voted to shut the fund down and distribute the metal, some shareholders will not receive metal. This is not a result of mismanagement or malfeasance on the part of management. This is because investors can short ETF shares without posting metal to the fund's trust account. As a simple illustration, suppose one ETF share equals ownership of 1 ounce of gold. A fund sells 100 shares to investors and dutifully buys 100 ounces of gold—so far, so good. However, some other investors believe the price of gold will decline and borrow 50 of the ETF shares and sell them short to 50 additional new investors, who now have long positions. The new investors don't know their shares came from speculators who borrowed the shares to take short positions.

Now, 150 investors are long shares and believe the fund is holding gold for them—when it is only holding 100 ounces of gold. If, for whatever reason, the fund is liquidated, 50 shareholders will not get gold. This disadvantage is solvable. The rules for shorting would have to change so that anyone who wants to short an ETF would have to borrow both an ETF share and an ounce of gold. The gold they borrowed would be deposited with the fund. If that requirement were in place, the fund in our example would hold 150 ounces of gold and have 150 long shares outstanding. The party that lent the "shorter" gold would take the risk of not having the gold returned—not the long ETF holder. The party lending the gold would know that it was assuming a risk. Concern about ETFs not having enough gold to cover the longs has caused many ETF investors to move from ETFs to physical gold. See Figure 9.4.

FIGURE 9.4

Shifting Preference to Owning Physical

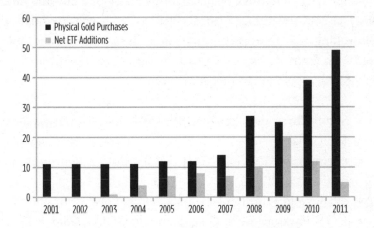

Other disadvantages to investing in ETF shares include:

- Should a government decide to seize gold, as the US government did in 1933, the large holdings of ETFs may prove to be irresistible. The reach of the US government extends beyond its shores.
- The low cost of trading ETF shares can lead to the temptation to trade excessively by trying to catch every fluctuation in the price of gold. This is dangerous and usually self-defeating. Precious metals should do well over the long term but can experience severe and completely unpredictable volatility

over the short term. Days when all the news would lead a rational thinker to expect gold to be up sharply, it will plunge. Buy metals with the idea of holding them for five years and you'll be fine.

Forms of ETFs

Gold ETFs come in three primary forms: those that buy and hold physical gold unleveraged, those that invest in gold by holding and rolling gold futures contracts, and those that buy and hold gold with leverage. Most ETF investors prefer to buy funds that hold physical gold unleveraged, including:

- Sprott Physical Gold Trust (PHYS)—Gold held in Canada: $2.7 billion
- iShares COMEX Gold Trust (IAU)—Gold held around the world: $15 billion
- SPDR Gold Trust (GLD)—Gold held in London: $75 billion
- ETFS Physical Swiss Gold Shares (SGOL)—Gold held in Switzerland: $2 billion
- ETFS Physical Asian Gold Shares (AGOL)—Gold held in Singapore: $150 million

While each of these ETFs has its own advantages and disadvantages, the one that's unique is the Sprott Physical Gold Trust:

- PHYS is technically a closed-end fund, and not an ETF, so US individual investors pay 0% to 23.8% capital gains tax, instead of the 28% collectibles tax on the profits from GLD and IAU.
- Like any closed-end fund, the fund shares may trade at a premium or discount to net asset value. If the shares trade at a

discount, the manager would buy them back and liquidate an equivalent amount of gold to lock in a risk-free profit for the remaining shareholders. When the shares do go to a high premium, a sign of excessive interest, the company can and has issued new shares, which lowers the premium. Beware of buying when the premium is high.

- The fund holds, in a fully segregated account at the Royal Canadian Mint, only serial numbered gold bars approved for delivery in London.
- PHYS is the only major ETF that allows investors to directly exchange units for physical gold—however, direct exchange results in a 28% tax instead of a 15% to 20% tax.
- The gold is held at a nonfinancial custodian (a government mint) and is not exposed, even indirectly, to the collapse of the banking system.

Other ETFs elect to hold and roll futures contracts on the metals. Examples of these ETFs include DGL PowerShares and E-TRACs CMCI Gold Total Return. The advantage these funds offer is that the gold doesn't actually have to be bought and stored—both of which are expensive and reduce return. The disadvantages are that:

- All these funds hold as assets are futures contracts from the exchange. These contracts do not promise that the long can actually receive physical gold. The volume of paper gold exceeds the amount of physical gold held for delivery by the exchange by a huge percentage. If more than a few percent of the investors who are long contracts actually want to take delivery, the exchange will not have enough gold. In this event, the longs receive cash instead. People don't buy gold ETFs to end up with cash.

- While in theory holding gold and/or rolling gold futures should offer the same return (otherwise there would be an arbitrage possibility), theory and reality sometimes diverge. For a variety of reasons, the futures contracts could deviate from their theoretical value and cause the futures to underperform the physical or vice versa. This results in greater deviations between gold's performance and the performance of the ELF.

The funds listed next are leveraged ETFs—leveraged two/three times:

- Proshares Ultra Gold (ETF)—2 × performance
- Proshares UltraShort Gold (ETF)—2 × performance
- Direxion Daily Gold Miners Bull Shares (ETF)
- Direxion Daily Gold Miners Bear 3 × Shares

All leveraged funds have the problem of their returns underperforming over the long term because their results are calculated on a geometric return basis. An example will illustrate. Suppose the price of gold declines 5% on one day and rises 5% the next. A triple leveraged fund would mean a 15% decline followed by a 15% gain—which gives the investor a net loss. The 15% gain is on 85% of the investor's original investment, not 100%. This is because the return is not a simple average. Instead, it is calculated:

$$[(1 + R_1) \times (1 + R_2) \times \ldots \times (1 + R_n)]^{1/n} - 1 = \text{Geometric Return}$$
$$[(1 + .15) \times (1 - .15)]^{1/2} - 1$$
$$[(1.15) \times (.850)]^{1/2} - 1 = -1.13\% \text{ per year}$$

Since $(a \times b) = (b \times a)$, it makes no difference if the gain comes before the loss or the loss comes before the gain.

Equity Linked Notes

An equity linked note is a note that pays a return tied to the change in the market price of gold. The advantage of ELNs is that they can be designed to offer different risk–reward trade-offs ranging from a highly leveraged reward–risk note to a note that has 70% of gold's upside but none of the downside. Each investor can choose the risk–reward ratio that is right for them. For example, a conservative investor might want a 5-year note that offers the following value proposition:

- If gold goes down, the investor still receives 100% of principal at maturity.
- If gold goes up, the investor receives principal plus 70% of gold's appreciation.

The dealer creates the note by combining a 5-year zero coupon note that the dealer issues and a 5-year note at-the-money (ATM) option on gold, as shown in Figure 9.5.

FIGURE 9.5

Creation of a 5-Year Principal Protected Note

5-Year ZCB + 5 Year ATM Option = 100% Principal
Protected Note

For example, an investor puts up $2 million. The dealer borrows $1,567,052 from the investor and issues the investor a 5-year, 5%, zero coupon note. The dealer then spends $432,948 to buy a 5-year at-the-money option on gold. Since $432,948 is 70% of the cost of a 5-year ATM call option on $2 million in gold, the investor gets a 70% participation rate. Therefore, if gold was $2,000 when the note was issued, Figure 9.6 shows the investor's return.

FIGURE 9.6

Return on Note vs. Gold

Value of Gold in 5 Years	Dollars Returned by Note per $2,000 Invested	Percent Return for Note	Percent Return for Gold Bullion
$500	$2,000	0%	−75%
$1,000	$2,000	0%	−50%
$2,000	$2,000	0%	0%
$3,000	$2,700	35%	50%
$4,000	$3,400	70%	100%
$5,000	$4,100	105%	250%
$6,000	$4,800	140%	400%

Even though ELNs require the purchase of options, it's the dealer who buys them, not the investor. The investor just buys a note. Therefore, ELNs can be purchased by investors who are prohibited from buying derivatives. The vast majority of gold-linked notes are in privately marketed deals that then trade over the counter. There are some publicly traded exceptions, including:

- Powershares Deutsche Bank Gold Double Long Equity Linked Note (DPG)
- Powershares Deutsche Bank Gold Double Short Equity Linked Note (DZZ)
- VelocityShares 3× Long Gold ETN (UGLD)
- VelocityShares 3× Inverse Gold ETN (DGLD)

Gold Stocks

Another, albeit indirect, way to own gold is to invest in gold stocks. Gold stocks fall into three general categories based upon the amount of ounces they produce each year:

- Senior (>500K)
- Intermediate (>100K and <500K)
- Junior (<100K)

Figure 9.7 lists the ten largest publicly traded mining companies.

FIGURE 9.7

The Ten Biggest Publicly Traded Gold Mining Companies

Name	Country	Market Capital ($B)
Barrick	Canada	27
Goldcorp	Canada	22
Newmont	United States	18
Newcrest	Australia	10
AngloGold	South Africa	12
Yamana	Canada	6
Kinross	Canada	11
Gold Fields	South Africa	7
Eldorado Gold	Canada	3
Polyus	Russia	9

Despite these companies being the world's largest mining companies, only six of them produce more than one million ounces per year. Of all the industries in the world, it is arguable that gold mining is one of the hardest industries in which to be successful. Consider the following:

- Man has sought gold for more than 10,000 years. The "low-hanging fruit" was found and mined out millennia ago. Today, in order to find gold, miners must overcome tremendous obstacles. Miners dive in the ice cold Bering Sea in Alaska and work in swamp-water-filled holes surrounded by poisonous snakes in the most remote sections of jungle in Ghana. For surface mines, the layers of dirt and stone that cover the gold-bearing gravel strata and must be removed before mining can even begin can be 30 to 80 feet thick. Mines that follow veins of gold that dive underground may have to dig shafts down 2.5 miles into the earth. At that depth, the temperature is over 130 degrees F.

- The attractiveness of the physical prospects is becoming less attractive. Miners used to have to process 1 ton of rock to obtain an ounce of gold. Now, on average, they have to process 2.5 tons of rock to obtain that same ounce of gold. This alone would raise their costs 250%—if those costs remained constant.

- Gold mining is capital intensive. The costs of acquiring mining rights, acquiring and moving the various excavation machines to the job site, water pumps, generators, processing plants, acquiring and moving the diesel fuel, insurance, and labor have all soared. These higher costs have raised the operational cost of extracting an ounce of gold from the low $300s to the high $900s. That's before taxes, survey costs, environmental studies, royalties, sharing arrangements, overhead, etc.

- Theft by employees and/or outsiders can be difficult and expensive to stop. Recently, a small mine in Mexico that was protected by four armed security guards was surrounded by 30 heavily armed men who stole an entire month's production. While losing a month's production was expensive, what was even more expensive for the industry is that every mine in Mexico then had to substantially boost their costs and armed security.

- Owning a claim doesn't guarantee the right to mine the claim. As shown on a TV reality show in the United States, two Americans bought the right to mine a claim in Guyana. When they showed up on their claim, there were 200 heavily armed Chinese illegally squatting on their claim and stripping it of resources. The government of Guyana was powerless to evict them.

- In addition to the risk of bandits robbing the mine is the risk that the host government will change the rules after the mining company has made a tremendous investment. Within the recent past Venezuela, Mongolia, Bolivia, and South Africa have all either nationalized mines or threatened to do so. Even governments that don't nationalize can still raise taxes and/or tariffs. Countries that have recently either raised taxes or have threatened to do so include Australia, Brazil, Tanzania, Peru, Sudan, Ivory Coast, and the United States. Currently, the United States charges nothing to mine on federal land, but a bill that imposes a 12.5% royalty is making its way through the US Congress.

- Environmental constraints are becoming increasingly costly. Few activities do more environmental damage than gold mining. Gold mining requires massive amounts of earth moving and massive quantities of water. It often generates run-off that can contaminate streams in the area for dozens of miles around. The cyanide or mercury used in the extraction process are both highly toxic. Complying with the increasingly strict environmental regulations and obtaining the often required environmental insurance is becoming far more difficult and more expensive.

- Long lead time also increases costs. Because of the studies that have to be performed and permits that have to be obtained, it is not uncommon for a decade to go by between the time the mining company acquires the right to mine some property and when the first shovelful of dirt is removed.

- Despite all the advances in technology, mining remains remarkably dangerous. Mines are always subject to cave-ins and flooding. Machines move back and forth rapidly with limited visibility. Who could forget the 33 Chilean miners who were trapped underground for 69 days?

- Mines are self-liquidating. Every mine eventually is depleted. Some of the mine's cash flow has to be used to try and acquire new prospects if the company is to continue. The cost of new prospects is rising and the number of new prospects that actually hold substantial gold reserves is declining, as illustrated in Figure 9.8.

Experienced mining engineers are in short supply and so tend to be very expensive ($250K and up). Given the remote locations and special risks, sometimes even basic labor is also quite expensive.

Despite the fact that the price of gold has more than tripled over the last decade and mining activity has exploded, the number of ounces mined each year has been very consistent. As existing mines are played out, new mines are brought on line—but they are far less productive than the mines they are replacing.

FIGURE 9.8

Number of Major New Gold Strikes

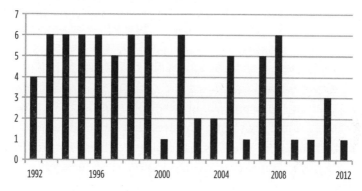

For all of these reasons, recently, the mining sector has dramatically underperformed the price of the metals. As always, this leads to two schools of thought. Some investors believe that the mining sector will continue to underperform both the market and the metal; others believe that the mining sector will catch up at some point.

The advocates for stocks instead of metals believe that owning the stocks offers three advantages: leverage, lower tax rates, and the opportunity for a pleasant surprise if it turns out the prospect holds more gold than anticipated. To invest in the senior gold miners, investors can pick individual stocks, buy mutual funds, or buy ETFs that buy the entire senior gold sector.

Valuing Individual Gold Stocks

Gold stocks must be valued two ways—first, as an operating company throwing off earnings, and second, as a "bank" holding gold. The shares are worth the greater of the two valuations.

As an operating company, a gold company produces a product, gold, which it produces at a cost and sells, hopefully at a profit. This is no different than a company that produces toothpaste, except for the following:

- A mining company cannot differentiate the price of its product from the competition: An 8-ounce tube of Crest may be worth more than an 8-ounce tube of Colgate, but all gold is of equal value.
- A mining company will only be able to produce its product for a limited time before the deposit is depleted.
- The amount of gold a mine produces declines over time while costs rise. It makes sense to mine the most lucrative section first and then move to progressively less productive areas until mining is no longer sufficiently profitable.
- Miners often have to pay a royalty to the landowner and/or financer.

For example, a mining company could, based on its analysis of the gold in its ground, have projections like those shown in Figure 9.9.

FIGURE 9.9

Valuation of a Mining Company

	1	2	3	4	5	6	7	8	9	10
Ounces Produced (000)	64	60	56	52	48	40	32	28	16	12
Expected Sale Price	$2,000	$2,050	$2,100	$2,150	$2,200	$2,250	$2,300	$2,350	$2,340	$2,345
Cost to Produce	$950	$1,050	$1,150	$1,250	$1,350	$1,450	$1,550	$1,650	$1,750	$1,850
Profit per Ounce	$1,050	$1,000	$950	$900	$850	$800	$750	$700	$590	$495
Total Profit (000)	$67,200	$60,000	$53,200	$46,800	$40,800	$32,000	$24,000	$19,600	$9,440	$5,940
Discount Rate	10%	10%	10%	10%	10%	10%	10%	10%	10%	10%
Present Value (000)	$61,091	$49,587	$39,970	$31,965	$25,334	$18,063	$12,316	$9,144	$4,003	$2,290
PV Total Profit	$253,762,000									

The projections shown in Figure 9.9 are for a company in liquidation. For an ongoing enterprise, a company would need a line showing some (or most likely a substantial) portion of its profits used to acquire new tracts to mine.

The second way to value a mining company is as a "gold bank." Some junior mining companies often have no intention of doing any actual mining. They lack the interest, the expertise, and/or the capital to do the actual mining. Instead, what they do is:

- Search for land that they hope will be relatively rich in gold deposits.
- Secure the rights to mine the land by either filing a claim or negotiating with the landowner.
- Run a series of core samples in order to assess the size and density of the gold deposit—in effect create the underground 3D map of the gold deposits (scope and density).
- If the property has the potential to cost-effectively produce:
  - More than 1 million ounces, the junior will then sell it to one of the majors. Particularly desirable are prospects adjacent to land already being mined by a senior gold miner.
  - Between 250,000 and 1 million ounces, the junior will look to take on a dedicated extraction firm as a partner. In other words, they will partner with a firm that specializes in digging, extraction, and fabrication.
  - Fewer than 250,000 ounces, the junior will look to sell to a wealthy family (to hold as "gold in the ground" as an investment for future generations) or to a small family mining operation.

Figure 9.10 lists the largest ETFs for gold miners.

FIGURE 9.10

Largest ETFs for Gold Miners

Market Vectors Gold Miners ETF	GDX
Global X Gold Explorers ETF	GLDX
ETFX Russell Global Gold Mining ETF	AUCO-FSE
iShares CDN Gold Sector Index Fund	XGD-TSX

Investing in mining stocks requires an expertise well beyond that of a typical broker or investment advisor. It requires specialists who eat, sleep, and dream about mines and mining. A good mining broker will visit dozens of mines each year, have contacts from the boardrooms to the truck operators, be able to recite the number of proven and probable ounces for each mine, and know each mine's cost of extraction per ounce.

Author's personal note: One such company is Strategic Energy Research and Capital, located in Summit, New Jersey, where the principals have 100 years of experience between them. Call George Ross at (908) 918-0900 for help selecting gold stocks.

ROYALTY TRUSTS

In a royalty trust, investors pool their funds and hire a management company, which then provides capital to mining companies. In exchange for providing the capital, the royalty trust receives either a predetermined number of ounces of gold or a percentage of the mine's total production. Royalty trusts don't do any actual mining; they strictly provide financing. When a mine runs short of capital, royalty trusts can often negotiate very favorable terms— for example, providing 10% of the overall capital in exchange for

25% of the mine's production. For royalty trust deals, timing is everything. Figure 9.11 lists some royalty trusts.

FIGURE 9.11

Gold Royalty Trusts

Name	Symbol
Royal Gold	RGLD
Franco-Nevada	FNNVF.PK
Enduro Royalty Trust	NDRO
Allied Nevada	ANV
International Royalty	ROY

GOLD IN THE GROUND

In addition to buying bullion, one clever strategy that wealthy families utilize is to buy nearly worthless desert land that they think may contain gold. Once they purchase the land, they have a complete set of core samples taken so that a 3D picture of the gold below the ground and a very accurate estimate of the number of recoverable ounces is prepared. Then, the family does nothing but pass the supposedly near worthless land from one generation to the next. After all, why go to the expense of digging and refining the gold— only then to rebury it in a vault. The gold is safer under thousands of tons of rock than it would be in any safe deposit box.

JEWELRY

Some investors prefer gold jewelry to coins or bullion. They like to get "double duty" out of their gold investments—being able to wear it while it stores their wealth and appreciates. The type of jewelry that appreciates the most falls into one of two categories:

- Bullion in disguise
- Masterpieces of a goldsmith's artistry

There are numerous manufacturers that make necklaces and bracelets that are thinly disguised bullion investments. In this case, the beads or bars are 24K or 22K yellow or white gold. One manufacturer allows buyers to choose whether the gold beads that comprise their necklace contain one-quarter, one-half, or one ounce of 22K gold. The buyer can specify how long the necklace should be. Because this jewelry requires a minimum amount of labor, it is priced at a slight premium over bullion, both when it is bought and when it is sold.

The second category is jewelry that is a masterpiece of goldsmith's artistry, such as the trademark panther bracelets by Cartier. Masterpieces of design that only employ the best materials and jewels should always hold their value in downturns and enjoy great appreciation over the long term.

Avoid jewelry that requires many man-hours of labor but that doesn't rise to the level of a masterpiece. Their resale value can fall sharply after purchase and take decades to recover.

By far the biggest market for gold jewelry is India. From the poor to the very rich, the people of India put a large portion of their savings into gold jewelry. Historically, Indians have had little opportunity to invest in stocks or bonds. The distrust between the people and the government has caused people to prefer hard assets. The traditionally high rate of inflation has also caused people to favor holding gold as an inflation hedge. Figure 9.12 shows the number of grams of gold held per unit of GDP in a variety of countries around the world.

FIGURE 9.12

Gold Demand in Grams per Unit of GDP

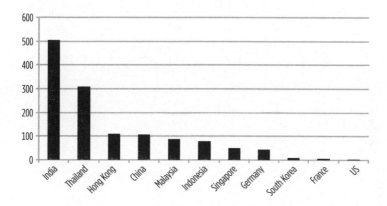

As Figure 9.12 indicates, relative to Asian populations, the US population spends comparatively nothing on jewelry relative to its GDP. The United States has the great potential growth market for jewelry as an investment vehicle.

CHAPTER TEN

Other Precious Metals

While gold may be the most popular precious metal, it is not the only one. Silver, platinum, and palladium are other noble metals that are sometimes used interchangeably with gold.

SILVER

The arguments that support the purchase of gold as an alternative investment apply to the purchase of silver. In addition, there are arguments for buying silver that apply to silver—but not gold—despite the fact that they are both precious metals:

- Silver is historically less expensive than gold. In the past, the price of 15 ounces of silver equaled the price of 1 ounce of gold. As of this writing, the exchange rate is approximately 50 to 1.
- 500 million ounces of silver are consumed per year in industrial applications including:

- Silver oxide batteries—which outperform lithium batteries
- Tableware and serving ware
- Water purification
- Contacts in switches
- Radiography
- Optical disk coatings
- Solar radiation protection
- Catalysts used in the production of numerous plastics and polymers
- Metal alloys
- Photovoltaic cells

■ Silver is usually not "cost effective" to recover so, unlike gold, most of the silver that's consumed eventually ends up in landfills.

■ Silver is affordable, so small silver coins can be used for typical small daily purchases.

■ Adding to the allure of silver is the belief held by some investors that the world consumes silver (850 million ounces year) at a higher rate than it is produced (650 million ounces year). It is estimated that the aboveground surplus will be exhausted in nine years. This suggests the future price will rise substantially. Note that there is no consensus about demand exceeding supply, since no one can agree on the actual number of ounces produced or consumed in a year.

■ Silver is also growing in popularity as an alternative asset class. Figure 10.1 shows the purchase of new silver coins from the US Mint over the last few years (in millions of ounces). That volume now exceeds the US annual silver production, so the United States has become a net importer of silver.

Ounces of Silver Purchased from the US Mint from 2000 Through 2012

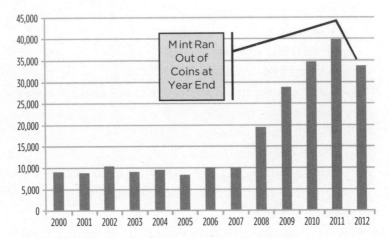

Silver's biggest disadvantages are that:

- It is bulky. Five hundred ounces of silver is currently worth about $17,500 and weighs 31.25 pounds. A million dollars' worth of silver, therefore, weighs about 1,800 pounds. That's a lot of weight to store and transport.
- It is very volatile. Its price is far more volatile than gold, as shown in Figure 10.2.

FIGURE 10.2

The High Volatility of Silver

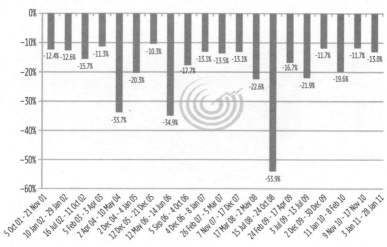

Source: Casey Research

Investing in Silver

Investors can buy silver in the same forms and products as gold, including physical silver, futures contracts, ETFs, ETNs, stocks, and so forth. One of the most popular ways to buy silver is in the Green Monster Box (shown in Figure 10.3), which is produced by the United States Mint and then sold to the public via a limited number of top tier dealers who are authorized to buy directly from the Mint.

FIGURE 10.3

A Box of 500 One-Ounce Silver Coins from the US Mint

Note that, in the futures market for silver, there sometimes occurs something unusual. Under normal circumstances, the later the expiration date for a futures contract, the higher the contract price. The price is higher as the expiration date extends because it costs more to store silver for a longer period of time. When the price becomes progressively higher as the expiration date extends, the market is said to be "contango." This is the normal state for the silver market. However, as shown in Figure 10.4, at times, future prices become lower as their maturity increases. This is called "backwardization" and is abnormal. Figure 10.4 suggests that there is a risk-free profit available.

For example, anyone who owned physical silver could simultaneously:

- Sell the silver in 2011 and receive the sales proceeds in cash.
- Invest the sales proceeds in an interest-bearing investment.
- Enter into futures contracts that allow them to buy the silver back in December of 2015 at a lower price.

Then, in December of 2015, the investor could buy back the silver at the price of the futures contract and make a risk profit. Look at Figure 10.4; someone with 1 million ounces could:

- Sell 1 million ounces in spot market at $35.60 per ounce—netting $35,600,000
- Enter into a contract to buy the silver back in December 2015 at $33.95 per ounce
- Invest the sales proceeds for 4 years and 4 months at 5% rendering P + I = $35,600,000 + ($35,600,000 × .05 × 4.33) = $43,307,400
- Fulfill the contract by buying the silver back in December of 2015 for $33,950,000
- Make a net profit of $9,357,400 (less fees and taxes)

FIGURE 10.4

Silver Futures in Backwardization

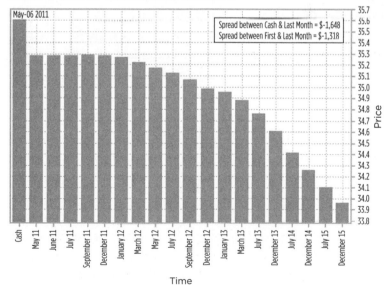

Source: sharelynx.com

The reason everyone who owns physical silver doesn't jump on this "opportunity" to make a profit is that investors are concerned that, if they sell their physical silver today, they won't be able to get it back in the future. This is because the amount of silver traded in the futures market dwarfs the amount of physical silver that the exchange actually has available in inventory to make deliveries.

Typically, very few of the investors who are long silver futures actually take delivery. At expiration, they close out their position for cash that is added to (or removed from) their margin account. Therefore, very few of the investors who short silver ever have to actually deliver physical silver. The futures exchange has no requirement that participants who short silver actually own silver that they can deliver. The exchange expects that for the 1% to 2% of contracts that do go to delivery, the "shorts" that don't have silver will be able to buy silver from the exchange at the then-current spot price. Once they buy it, they can deliver the silver.

However, if there is some kind of a crisis and 50% of those who are long futures contracts want to take delivery of silver, there will not be enough silver to fulfill all the delivery requests. Once the silver in inventory is exhausted, the buy orders are settled in cash (at the last price the future traded) instead of with the actual metal. Thus, investors who sell their silver today may not be able to get it back if there is some kind of a financial or political crisis. As was the case with gold, China is a wild card. Over the past few years, China has gone from being a net exporter of silver to being a huge importer, as shown in Figure 10.5.

FIGURE 10.5

Silver Accumulations in China

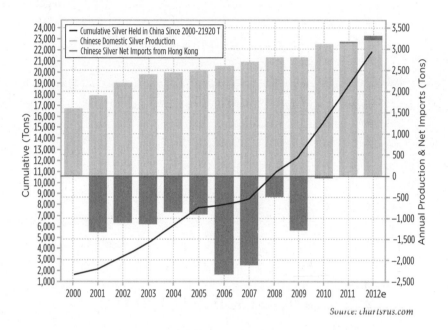

Source: chartsrus.com

For all of the reasons discussed earlier in this chapter, silver outperformed gold, as well as all other asset classes, from November of 2008 to November of 2012, as shown in Figure 10.6. As was the case with gold, the biggest driver behind the price increase is increased buying by China. China went from being a large exporter through Hong Kong (2001 to 2009) to being a huge importer. Again, the official figures may understate the true increase because the Chinese government figures are always questionable.

FIGURE 10.6

Performance of Silver over the Last Three Years

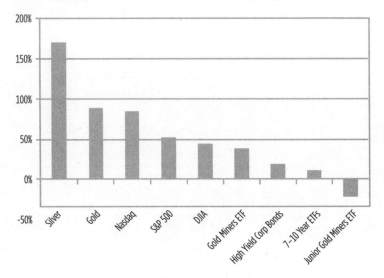

Platinum and Palladium

Platinum and palladium are the two other noble metals that also are suitable as alternative investments. Like gold and silver, they are used as jewelry and have industrial applications. These metals are used primarily:

- In catalytic converters to mitigate carbon monoxide pollution by acting as a catalyst to convert it into carbon dioxide
- To line vats in order to make them acid-proof

Arguments for platinum over gold are that:

- Platinum is 20 times rarer than gold, yet is priced similarly.
- Platinum is only found in sizeable deposits in four places:

- South Africa in the Bushveld Igneous Complex (65% of annual production)
- Russia's Norilsk-Talnakh mines in the Ural Mountains (15% of annual production)
- Canada's Sudbury Basin (10% of annual production)
- Other locations, usually the locations of meteor strikes—the moon and meteors have high platinum and palladium concentrations (10% of annual production)

From a western perspective, the suppliers of platinum and palladium are unreliable for the following reasons:

- The Russian government could simply refuse to sell the metal to the west as part of the ongoing geopolitical structure.
- The South African government is unstable and its miners are unhappy. Recent labor strikes have resulted in hundreds of deaths and put the entire mining industry in South Africa at risk.

Rare Earth and Strategic Metals

Some of the so-called rare earth metals are rarer than the precious metals. They usually are not mined separately; instead, they are often the by-products of other mining operations. Each of these metals has key industrial applications, as described in Figure 10.7.

FIGURE 10.7

Uses of Rare Earth Metals

Rhodium	Plate for platinum jewelry to give it shine
	Catalytic converters for 2 NO_2 to O_2 plus N_2 conversion
Antimony	Tracer bullets, infrared detectors
	Hardened lead, cable sheathing
Bismuth	Fire alarms (low melting point)
	Medication (hemorrhoid creams)
Cadmium	NiCd batteries
	PVC pipe
Cobalt	Powerful magnets
	Strong steels for jet turbines
Gallium	Mirrors
	Convert electricity into light
Germanium	Fluorescent lights
	Transistors
Indium	Mirrors
	Photocells
Molybdenum	Tempered steel
	High temperature steels
Rhenium	Filaments for mass spectrometers
	Superconductors
Selenium	Printer toner
	Semiconductors
Vanadium	Binds titanium to steel
	Nuclear reactors
Dysprosium	Cruise missiles
	Flat screens

The only practical way to invest in rare metal is via an ETF, such as the Market Vectors Rare Earth Strategic Metals ETF (REMX). China has a near monopoly on some the rare earth metals and has threatened to cease exports in violation of the World Trade Organization's rules.

Precious Metal Quotes

Irredeemable paper money has almost invariably proved a curse to the country employing it.

—IRVING FISHER

Paper currencies always reach their intrinsic value, which is zero.

—VOLTAIRE

Coinage is imprinted gold or silver, by which the prices of things bought and sold are reckoned. . . . It is therefore a measure of values. A measure, however, must always preserve a fixed and constant standard. Otherwise, public order is necessarily disturbed, with buyers and sellers being cheated in many ways, just as if the yard, bushel, or pound did not maintain an invariable magnitude.

—COPERNICUS

Of all the contrivances for cheating the laboring class of mankind, none has been more effective than that which deludes them with paper money.

—DANIEL WEBSTER

The most important thing about money is to maintain its stability. . . . You have to choose between trusting to the natural stability of gold and the natural stability and intelligence of the members of the government. And with due respect to these gentlemen, I advise you, as long as the capitalist system lasts, to vote for gold.

—GEORGE BERNARD SHAW

Lenin was certainly right. There is no subtler, no surer means of overturning the existing basis of society than to debauch the currency. The process engages all the hidden forces of economic law on the side of destruction, and does it in a manner which not one man in a million can diagnose.

—JOHN MAYNARD KEYNES

The first panacea for a mismanaged nation is inflation of the currency; the second is war. Both bring a temporary prosperity: both bring permanent ruin. But both are the refuge of political and economic opportunists.

—ERNEST HEMINGWAY

Gold and economic freedom are inseparable. The abandonment of the gold standard made it possible for the welfare statists to use the banking system as a means to an unlimited expansion of credit. . . . The financial policy of the welfare state requires that there be no way for the owners of wealth to protect themselves. This is the shabby secret of the welfare statists' tirades against gold. Deficit spending is simply a scheme for the confiscation of wealth. Gold stands in the way of this insidious process. It stands as a protector of property rights.

—ALAN GREENSPAN

[Currency devaluation] occasions a general and most pernicious subversion of the fortunes of private people; enriching in most cases the most idle and profuse debtor at the expense of the industrious and frugal creditor, and transporting a great part of the national

capital from the hands that were likely to increase and improve it, to those which are likely to dissipate and destroy it.

—ADAM SMITH

Gold is money. Everything else is credit.

—J. P. MORGAN

No nation in history has ever survived fiat money, money that did not have precious metal backing.

—RONALD REAGAN

No other commodity enjoys as much universal acceptability and marketability as gold.

—HANS SENNHOLZ

In the long run, the gold price has to go up in relation to paper money. There is no other way. To what price, that depends on the scale of the inflation—and we know that inflation will continue.

—NICHOLAS DEAK

If ever there was an area in which to do the exact opposite of that which government and the media urge you to do, that area is the purchasing of gold.

—ROBERT RINGER

Gold is steady as a rock, a standard bearer by which all currencies can be accurately measured.

—MARK SKOUSEN

For more than two thousand years, gold's natural qualities made it man's universal medium of exchange. In contrast to political money, gold is honest money that survived the ages and will live on long after the political fiats of today have gone the way of all paper.

—HANS SENNHOLZ

Gold is forever. It is beautiful, useful, and never wears out. Small wonder that gold has been prized over all else, in all ages, as a store of value that will survive the travails of life and the ravages of time.

—JAMES BLAKELY

As fewer and fewer people have confidence in paper as a store of value, the price of gold continues to rise.

—JEROME SMITH

Gold would have value if for no other reason than that it enables a citizen to fashion his financial escape from the state.

—WILLIAM RICKENBACKER

The desire for gold is the most universal and deeply rooted commercial instinct of the human race.

—GERALD LOEB

When paper money systems begin to crack at the seams, the run to gold could be explosive.

—HARRY BROWNE

Gold was not selected arbitrarily by governments to be the monetary standard. Gold had developed for many centuries on the free market as the best money; as the commodity providing the most stable and desirable monetary medium.

—MURRAY ROTHBARD

Gold bears the confidence of the world's millions, who value it far above the promises of politicians, far above the unbacked paper issued by governments as money substitutes. It has been that way through all recorded history. There is no reason to believe it will lose the confidence of people in the future.

—OAKLEY BRAMBLE

With the exception only of the period of the gold standard, practically all governments of history have used their exclusive power to issue money to defraud and plunder the people.

—F. A. VON HAYAK

Nothing beats a little cash in a bear market, of course, and the oldest form of cash is gold.

—JAMES GRANT

Even during the period when Rome lost much of her ancient prestige, an Indian traveler observed that trade all over the world was operated with the aid of Roman gold coins which were accepted and admired everywhere.

—PAUL EINZIG

To prefer paper to gold is to prefer high risk to lower risk, instability to stability, inflation to steady long-term values, a system of very low grade performance to a system of higher, though not perfect performance.

—WILLIAM REES-MOGG

The modern mind dislikes gold because it blurts out unpleasant truths.

—JOSEPH SCHUMPETER

The gold standard, in one form or another, will prevail long after the present rash of national fiats is forgotten or remembered only in currency museums.

—HANS SENNHOLZ

Although gold and silver are not by nature money, money is by nature gold and silver.

—KARL MARX

Gold is worshipped in all climates, without a single temple, and by all classes, without a single hypocrite.

—CALEB COLTON

Betting against gold is the same as betting on governments. He who bets on governments and government money bets against 6,000 years of recorded human history.

—GARY NORTH

The great merit of gold is precisely that it is scarce; that its quantity is limited by nature; that it is costly to discover, to mine, and to process; and that it cannot be created by political fiat or caprice.

—HENRY HAZLITT

Whenever an overall breakdown of a monetary or financial system occurs, return to gold always restores order, revives confidence and brings back prosperity.

—DONALD HOPPE

From a strictly economic point of view, buying gold in a major inflation and holding it probably presents the least risk of capital loss of any investment or speculation.

—HENRY HAZLITT

There are about three hundred economists in the world who are against gold, and they think that gold is a barbarous relic—and they might be right. Unfortunately, there are three billion inhabitants of the world who believe in gold.

—JANOS FEKETE

The history of paper money is an account of abuse, mismanagement, and financial disaster.

—RICHARD EBELING

There can be no other criterion, no other standard than gold. Yes, gold which never changes, which can be shaped into ingots, bars, coins, which has no nationality and which is eternally and universally accepted as the unalterable fiduciary value par excellence.

—CHARLES DE GAULLE

I see a great future for gold and silver coins as the currency people may increasingly turn to when paper currencies begin to disintegrate.

—MURRAY ROTHBARD

Start now buying gold coins, any kind, and hoarding them.

—JOHN L. KING

The gold standard makes the determination of money's purchasing power independent of the changing ambitions and doctrines of political parties and pressure groups. This is not a defect of the gold standard; it is its main excellence.

—LUDWIG VON MISES

It is extraordinary how many emotional storms one may weather in safety if one is ballasted with ever so little gold.

—WILLIAM MCFEE

Gold has worked down from Alexander's time. . . . When something holds good for two thousand years I do not believe it can be so because of prejudice or mistaken theory.

—BERNARD BARUCH

Under the placid surface, there are disturbing trends: huge imbalances, disequilibria, risks—call them what you will. Altogether, the circumstances seem to me as dangerous and intractable as any I can remember, and I can remember quite a lot. What really concerns me is that there seems to be so little willingness or capacity to do much about it. . . . We are skating on thin ice.

—PAUL VOLCKER

We live in a globalized environment and in a country which has enormous fiscal and external deficits. So you have to figure out some way—which I have not done I might add—to protect yourself if we should have a real currency problem here.

—ROBERT RUBIN

The planter, the farmer, the mechanic, and the laborer form the great body of the people yet they are in constant danger of losing their fair influence in the government. The mischief springs from the power which the money interest derives from a paper currency which they are able to control.

—ANDREW JACKSON

Government is the only agency that can take a valuable commodity like paper—slap some ink on it and make it worthless.

—LUDWIG VON MISES

Money, when considered as the fruit of many years' industry, as the reward of labor, sweat, and toil, as the widow's dowry and children's portion, and as the means of procuring the necessaries and alleviating the afflictions of life, and making old age a scene of rest, has something in it sacred that is not to be sported with, or trusted to the airy bubble of paper currency.

—THOMAS PAINE

You cannot legislate the poor into freedom by legislating the wealthy out of freedom. What one person receives without working for, another person must work for without receiving. The government cannot give to anybody anything that the government does not take from someone else. When half of the people get the idea they do not have to work because the other half is going to take care of them, and when the other half get the idea it does no good to work because someone else is going to get what they work for, that, my dear friend is the end of any nation. You cannot multiply wealth by dividing it.

—ADRIAN ROGERS

Whenever destroyers appear among men, they start by destroying money, for money is men's protection and the base of a moral existence. Destroyers seize gold and leave to its owners a counterfeit pile of paper. This kills all objective standards and delivers men into the arbitrary power of an arbitrary setter of values. Gold was an objective value, an equivalent of wealth produced. Paper is a mortgage on wealth that does not exist, backed by a gun aimed at those who are expected to produce it. Paper is a check drawn by legal looters upon an account which is not theirs: upon the virtue of the victims. Watch for the day when it bounces, marked, "Account overdrawn."

—AYN RAND

CHAPTER ELEVEN

Investing in Jewels

After precious metals, one of the most common alternative investments is fine jewels. The return on fine jewels has rivaled that of the stock and commodity markets, and jewels offer many of the same advantages of precious metals, including:

- They are very compact and so are efficient to store and transport.
- The supply is increasing at a lower and lower rate. Today's new mines are producing fewer and fewer jewels as new mines are less productive than the ones that are exhausted.
- The demand is increasing; as the number of middle class, wealthy, and very wealthy increase, so does the demand for fine jewels.

Jewels offer some major advantages that precious metals don't, including:

- You can wear and enjoy them; you can't wear a Green Monster Box of silver (a 500 coin box) to the theater.

- You have virtually no risk of government confiscation; the US government may confiscate gold again and perhaps even silver—but it won't confiscate jewels.

To view an excellent inventory of gems for sale, visit pioneergem .com. This site is maintained by one of the great gentlemen of the jewel market, Ed Nowak.

Jewels also offer some major disadvantages that precious metals don't, including:

- **Pricing**—Gold and silver have one price that is updated in real time around the world. With a minimum of comparison shopping among reputable dealers, it's easy to get a fair bid or offer on bars, coins, and bullion. Each jewel, however, is unique. Even if 5 carat white sapphires are trading on average at $1,000 per carat, an individual stone could be worth as little as $500 or as much as $2,500 per carat depending upon the stone's individual characteristics.
- **Liquidity**—Jewels are far less liquid than precious metals and are only suitable as long-term investments. The bid-ask spread is 10% to 20% for a careful shopper. Although the markup is high, gem prices can rise by 30% to 40% in a single year. Over the long term, spectacular stones have proven to be a spectacular investment.
- **Treatments**—Almost every variety of gemstone has possibly been subjected to treatments intended to improve its appearance.
  - Heating is the most common treatment. Heating a gemstone can melt away some inclusions and make the color more vivid. An unheated stone of the same size can be worth a multiple of the value of a heated stone. A qualified lab can test and determine whether a stone has been heated.

- Irradiation is used to cause stones to change color.
- Micro drill and fill can be used to remove inclusions.
- Oiling can make the surface shine.

Treatments, such as irradiation, that permanently alter a stone are considered acceptable. Those treatments that create a change that dissipates over time, like heating a ruby to temporarily intensify the color, are considered unacceptable and can severely impact the value of the jewel.

DIAMONDS

Because of their near monopoly on the engagement ring market, more western households own diamonds than any other gemstone. Engagement rings used to be set with sapphires, but diamonds are double refractive and their brilliance caused them to become the preferred stone for engagement rings.

Diamond purchasing is usually a traumatic experience for buyers because their knowledge is limited and the cost difference between different sizes and grades of diamonds can be so dramatic. Before shopping, everyone should become familiar with the 5Cs:

- Cut
- Clarity
- Color
- Carat weight
- Certificate

Cut

For diamonds, the most important "C" is the cut. This is because the brilliance of a diamond is dependent upon how well the diamond is cut. In a perfect cut, the light that enters from the top is reflected inside then back out the top. If the depth is too shallow or too deep, light leaks out the side of the diamond.

Cuts are evaluated as:

- **Ideal**—In an ideal cut, the table (flat area on the top) is as small as it can be—and still have 180-degree refraction out the top. This provides for an efficiency of diamond size and concentrates all the reflected light in a small table for maximum brilliance. The width and height of the refraction area are exactly equal—allowing in the maximum amount of light to be reflected. Most major diamond sellers have created trademark names for ideal cut diamonds:
  - At Blue Nile diamonds, it's the "Signature Ideal"
  - At Jared Jewelry, it's the "Leo Diamond"
  - At Ritani Jewelry, it's the "Ritani Reserve"
- **Premium**—In a premium cut diamond, the table is bigger, so the reflected light is spread over a larger area, reducing the brilliance but almost all the light still goes out the top.
- **Very good**—In this case, the cut is slightly sacrificed to create a larger diamond. The diamond could be cut down to a smaller, more ideal cut, but the loss of carat weight would reduce the stone's value more than improved cut would increase the stone's value.
- **Good**—Like a very good cut, the cut is sacrificed for carat weight, but to a greater degree.
- **Fair**—The fair cut was designed to maximize size without regard to brilliance.

Note that how good the cut is can be mathematically/scientifically determined and so is no longer a matter of opinion. (See the "Certificate" section later in this chapter.)

Clarity

The next is clarity. A perfect stone has no inclusions or flaws either internally, or on the surface of the stone. As with cut, there is a scale to measure clarity. To assess clarity, the stone must always be removed from the setting, since any competent jeweler will use the prongs of the setting to hide or at least minimize any flaws.

The clarity scale includes:

- **F**—Flawless.
- **IF**—Internally flawless. The stone has one or more surface flaws which may be hidden by a setting.
- **VVS1**—Very slightly included. The flaws are barely visible under 10× magnification by a trained gemologist.
- **VVS2**—Very slightly included. The flaws are visible under 10× magnification by a trained gemologist; the inclusions are larger than VVS1.
- **VS1**—Very slightly included. The flaws are visible to the untrained eye under 10× magnification. The inclusions are larger than VVS2.
- **VS2**—Very slightly included. The flaws are visible to the untrained eye under 10× magnification. The inclusions are larger than VS1.
- **SI1**—Minutely included. A few inclusions are easily visible under 10× magnification.
- **SI2**—Minutely included. More inclusions are easily visible under 10× magnification.
- Lower ranks include visible flaws and are not suitable as investments.

Diamonds with inclusions are often drilled to remove the inclusion and improve its appearance. The hole and shaft are then replaced with a polymer. Likewise, surface flaws are often filled with polymer. One question to ask about any diamond is, "Has it been subjected to any repairs or treatments?"

Color

White diamonds are ranked based on their absence of color, with colorless being the most valuable. (Note that this doesn't apply to fancy—colored—diamonds.)

D-rated diamonds are absolutely colorless—with higher letters meaning more color.

Take a look at Figure 11.1 to see what diamond buyers are buying. Most buyers are purchasing stones that have inclusions that are not visible and that, while appearing colorless to the naked eye, are not colorless. In other words, most buyers are not paying for improved quality that is not visible. That said, there will always be those buyers who want "perfect stones."

FIGURE 11.1

The Current Market for Diamonds

	Clarity						
Color	FL/IF	VVS1	VVS2	VS1	VS2	SI1	SI2
D	2%	1%	1%	1%	2%	2%	1%
E	1%	2%	3%	2%	5%	3%	2%
F	1%	2%	4%	5%	6%	3%	2%
G	1%	1%	1%	3%	6%	5%	2%
H	0%	0%	1%	2%	5%	4%	2%
I	0%	0%	1%	2%	3%	2%	2%
J	0%	0%	0%	1%	2%	1%	1%

Source: Blue Nile Diamonds

Carat Weight

For investment purposes, there are two strategies that make sense:

- Buy the single most perfect diamond you can afford—a 5-carat, D-Flawless, ideal cut looks good in anyone's portfolio.
- Buy ten to thousands of stones slightly less than 1 carat (VS1, VS2) (F, G, H). These are the most commonly used stones for engagement rings and, as such, should be the easiest to resell.

Special Issues

Diamonds are not as rare as most people think—particularly in the less than 1 carat size. Part of the diamond's allure was that their value was managed by DeBeers, which was owned by the Oppenheimer family. For all practical purposes, DeBeers was a worldwide monopoly and only released so many stones to the market. After losing some class action lawsuits that accused the firm of being a monopoly, the firm was sold to Anglo American. There is some question as to whether Anglo will be as effective at managing supply and controlling prices.

High-end buyers have begun a trend away from putting diamonds in engagement rings. Ever since Prince William gave Catherine his mother's sapphire ring as an engagement ring, there has been an emerging trend to use stones other than diamonds for engagement rings. High-quality sapphires, emeralds, rubies, and alexandrite are also being used.

DeBeers had an extremely effective marketing and advertising campaign. Tag lines like "A diamond is forever" and "Tell her you love her with two months' salary" are examples of advertising that was so effective they became part of advertising lore. It will be interesting to see if Anglo American will be as creative!

Fake Diamonds

When something the size of a pecan can cost more than $1 million, it is not surprising that people would try to fake them. The fakes range from crass and crude imitations to elegant replacements that only an expert jeweler can identify. The fakes fall into three categories:

- **Cubic zirconia and moissanite**—Cubic zirconia is the cubic crystalline form of zirconium dioxide (ZrO_2); moissanite is silicon carbide (SiC). They are easily recognizable (at close range). The stones are denser than diamond. Fifty million carats (10 tons) a year are manufactured.
- **Other clear natural stones**—Aragonite, bytownite, cerussite, danburite, datolite, dolomite, enstatite, fibrolite, forsterite, white garnet, herderite, iolite, jeremejevite, montebrasite, oligoclase, pargasite, phenakite, pollucite, scapolite, scheelite, sillimanite, and others can be (and probably have been) substituted for diamonds. They all have different chemical compositions but can be cut to look like diamonds.
- **Laboratory diamonds**—The Diamond Nexus, a diamond produced in a laboratory, comes the closest to true diamonds in brilliance, dispersion, and refraction. They have a different chemical composition (ten elements, as opposed to simply carbon) but are the hardest to differentiate from true flawless diamonds.

FIGURE 11.2

GIA Certificate

GEMOLOGICAL INSTITUTE OF AMERICA®

5355 Armada Drive | Carlsbad, CA 92008-4502
T: 760-603-4500 | F: 760-603-1814

GIA Laboratories
Bangkok   Carlsbad   Gaborone
Johannesburg   Mumbai   New York

www.gia.edu

ALEXANDRITE REPORT

November 28, 2012

GIA REPORT 2155124979

Weight	7.20 carat
Measurements	11.55 x 9.81 x 7.62 mm
Shape	Oval
Cutting Style: Crown	Brilliant Cut
Cutting Style: Pavilion	Step Cut
Transparency	Transparent
Color	Bluish Green changing to Purple

CONCLUSION

Species	NATURAL CHRYSOBERYL
Variety	ALEXANDRITE

Comments:
None

Image is Approximate

2155124979

IMPORTANT LIMITATIONS ON BACK
©2008 GEMOLOGICAL INSTITUTE OF AMERICA, INC.

Certificates

Unless you are an expert, when buying a used car you want to see the Carfax report, which details the car's history and any repairs. Likewise, when buying a diamond of any size, buyers should ask for a report from one of the larger and more prestigious gem labs that ranks the other 4 Cs. That will make it much easier to comparison shop. Figure 11.2 shows a facsimile of a certificate prepared by the Gemological Institute of America (GIA).

Once a diamond has been purchased, a tiny laser can etch a unique ID number onto the side of the diamond that identifies it. The owner's name is then stored in a database. This makes it easier to trace and recover the diamond if it is lost or stolen, but also lowers the anonymity of the owner.

COLORED GEMSTONES

Other gemstones also have the same Cs, but the emphasis on each C is different. For colored stones, not surprisingly, the color is the most important "C." Color is broken down into several components:

- **Consistent**—Is the color consistently deep from one end of the stone to the other or does the color get lighter from one side to the other? Consistent color is preferred, especially if it is a unique color.
- **Saturation**—Is the color vivid or washed out? The saturation should be even throughout the stone.
- **Hue**—Is the color defined along a color gradient in terms of red, green, or magenta? Some hues, such as royal blue and purple for sapphires, are preferred.

- **Transparency**—Can you see through the stone (transparent), partially see though the stone (translucent), or not see through the stone (opaque)? Transparency should also be consistent.

Carats

When investing in colored gemstones, buy the biggest and the best you can afford. Colored stones increase in price as their quality rises and as their size increases. Size is self-explanatory. Quality means free of inclusions, a beautiful color, complete transparency (when appropriate), no evidence of unacceptable treatments, and a cut that brings out the best in a stone. Quality is surprisingly easy to recognize. It doesn't take a gemologist. Put 50 similarly sized rubies, emeralds, or blue sapphires on a flat white or black background and ask people off the street, in succession, to select the "best one." They will almost always select the same three or four stones, over and over. Those three or four stones that people naturally select will always be the best of the lot. The human eye is very discerning and is drawn to the best quality stones.

The divergence between the price of small average natural stones and exceptionally large natural stones has been widening. Part of this divergence mirrors the concentration of wealth in society. As the top 1% of the population has acquired a greater percentage of the world's wealth, the price of the best of everything (restaurant meals, condos, yachts, art, cars, mansions, and the like) has also exploded upwards.

Finished colored stones come in two forms:

- **Faceted**—Faceted is currently the more common form; the stones are cut to maximize brilliance and reflection like diamonds.

- **Cabochon**—A cabochon is a smooth stone. Think of a ball or a football cut in half. These stones are less popular today, but tastes rotate, and these will be back in favor again.

There are dozens of different gemstones to choose from. Some are very rare and incredibly expensive; others are fairly common and quite reasonable in terms of price. Some of the most popular gemstones are listed in Figure 11.3.

FIGURE 11.3

Selected Gemstones for Collectors

Sapphires	Emeralds	Rubies	Alexandrites
Spinels	Tanzanites	Aquamarines	Garnets
Topazes	Apatites	Tourmalines	Amethysts
Zircons	Fluorides	Oligoclases	Opals

The next sections provide a few notes on each.

Sapphires

Sapphires are the second hardest gemstone. Sapphires are a form of aluminum oxide (AL_2O_3, also called corundum) with traces of other elements that change the color. Add a trace of cobalt and you get a blue sapphire. Add a trace of chromium and you get a red sapphire—also called a ruby. Other trace elements result in pink, yellow, rose, orange (aka padparadscha), green, and a unique variety that changes color in different types of light.

While sapphires come in a rainbow of colors, the most famous are the blue sapphires from:

- **Burma**—Burmese stones are often a classic royal blue.
- **Kashmir**—Stones from Kashmir include many microscopic

inclusions that diffuse light as it passes through the stone. This gives the stone a warm, sleepy look as opposed to a sharp, cold look.

- **Montana, United States**—US stones include the Yogo sapphires that have a lighter "cornflower blue," and that many regard the prettiest sapphire.

Sapphires range from transparent to opaque; those that are opaque are less valuable.

As an investment, fine sapphires are expected to slightly outperform the average gemstone. This means an appreciation of 20% to 25% per year.

Rubies

Ruby is another form of corundum that is very brilliant, very hard, and red. In large sizes, rubies are rarer than diamonds. Burmese rubies are considered the best due to their rich color, which results from high iron content.

As an investment, rubies are expected to underperform the average gemstone. This means an appreciation of 5% to 15% per year.

Emeralds

Emeralds are always green, although they do range from blue-green to intense dark green. Emeralds almost always have inclusions, so internally flawless stones are immediately suspected of being fakes. Colombia produces the finest emeralds. Almost all emeralds are oiled to increase their shine. While oiling is considered an acceptable practice, the stones may have to be renewed every few years.

As an investment, emeralds are expected to underperform the average gemstone. This means an appreciation of 5% to 15% per year.

Alexandrites

Alexandrite is a very rare stone that changes color from green in daylight to red/blue in incandescent light or candlelight. It is like owning an emerald during the day that becomes a sapphire or ruby by night. The stone was discovered in Russia's Ural Mountains and is named for Russian Tsar Alexander II. It is so rare that only one in a hundred thousand women will be able to own it. Most pieces are a half carat or less, with large stones being especially rare. Since this stone is so valuable, it is always cut to maximize the size of the stone over the shine.

As an investment, alexandrite is expected to substantially outperform the average gemstone. This means an appreciation of 30% to 45% per year.

Spinels

Spinel is one of the rarest gemstones. It comes in a variety of colors, with red currently being the most desirable. Spinels are almost always untreated. They are formed with rubies and are often mistaken for rubies.

As an investment, spinels are expected to outperform the average gemstone. This means an appreciation of 15% to 25% per year.

Amethysts

Amethyst is a purple variety of quartz. It is relatively common since large deposits were discovered in Zambia. It is an excellent value and currently large quality stones are readily available. Prices range from $10 to $30 per carat, based on the cut and color saturation. Amethysts should be eye clean and well cut.

As an investment, amethysts are expected to perform as the average gemstone. This means an appreciation of 10% to 20% per year.

Tanzanites

Tanzanite is a rich brilliant stone with colors that range between blue and purple. Under the right light, high-quality tanzanite emits red flashes. It was only discovered in 1967. In its natural state, tanzanite is an unattractive brown color. Tanzanite has been found in only one location, along Mt. Kilimanjaro in Tanzania. Superstition is that the gem was only found after a fire at the base of the mountain caused some brown pebbles to turn blue.

Today all tanzanite is heated. Since the color change is permanent, heating is an acceptable treatment. Tanzanite is a sleeper in terms of value. The mining is about exhausted and, while large stones (10 carats to 30 carats) were readily available, today they are becoming rarer. For investors with a 10 year to 15 year investment horizon, high-quality tanzanite may prove to be the best gemstone investment.

As an investment, tanzanites are expected to outperform almost every gemstone. This means an appreciation of 15% to 40% per year.

Aquamarines

Aquamarine is one of the most beautiful gemstones. Its light blue color is very appealing. Like tanzanite, it is almost always heat treated. Aquamarines are at their best in the 10 carat to 30 carat range.

As an investment, aquamarines are expected to slightly outperform the average gemstone. This means an appreciation of 20% to 25% per year.

Topazes

Topaz comes from Brazil and has a range of colors from yellow-brown to dull red-green. The surface is more muted than brilliant. Some designers refer to topazes as the perfect jewels to accompany fall colors. Topaz is not particularly rare or expensive and looks best in incandescent light or candlelight. They are found around the world, but the bulk come from Brazil.

As an investment, topaz is expected to slightly outperform the average gemstone. This means an appreciation of 20% to 25% per year.

Garnets

Like sapphires, garnets come in multiple colors. They are softer than sapphires but just as beautiful. Here are a few of the varieties:

- Garnet pyrope is a rich red
- Garnet spessartite ranges from orange to red brown.
- Garnet tsavorite is green.
- Garnet malaysia an orange honey pink color.

As an investment, garnets are expected to slightly outperform the average gemstone. This means an appreciation of 20% to 25% per year.

Tourmalines

Again, these stones come in many colors. Many people find them to be more attractive than the better known gemstones. Green tourmalines are more attractive than almost all emeralds, and the red ones outshine most rubies. It is for this reason that tourmalines are the other sleeper gem and are expected to dramatically outperform. Why buy a heavily included emerald when for the same price you can get bigger, shinier, eye clean tourmaline that doesn't need oiling?

Tourmalines show up best in sunlight and so are sometimes referred to as "day stones."

As an investment, tourmalines are expected to outperform the average gemstone. This means an appreciation of 30% to 45% per year with some potential for even faster growth.

Opals

Australia is the primary source for opals. They come with either white or black backgrounds. The black backgrounds show off the color better and so are usually preferred—all other factors being equal. The value of an opal is determined by:

- How bright the colors are
- How many colors there are
- The distribution of the colors

As an investment, opals are expected to underperform the average gemstone. This means an appreciation of 5% to 15% per year.

PEARLS

Before leaving the subject of gemstones, it is important to mention pearls, which many people consider to be another type of gemstone. They are the second most commonly owned type of jewelry and have been collected for over 4,000 years old.

Understanding Pearls

When a mollusk has an irritant—either a natural irritant or an irritant intentionally introduced by a pearl technician—the mollusk responds by first coating the irritant with a black substance called conchiolin. Then, the mollusk adds layer after layer of a whitish substance called nacre. The more layers of nacre that are added, the larger and more beautiful the pearl becomes. The value of a string of pearls is determined by many factors including:

- **The thickness of the nacre**—Fine pearls have layer after layer of nacre that took the mollusk years to lay over a small irritant. Cheap pearls have a thin layer of nacre laid over a large irritant. In some cases, the nacre is so thin that it wears away in a year or two. You can't rush the pearl-creating process.

- **The quality of the nacre**—In some cases, the nacre layers don't crystallize properly because the mollusk is moved or disturbed. In other cases, the layers are not uniform, thick at some points and thin at others, and a lopsided pearl is created.

- **The luster and orient of the nacre**—The luster and orient of the nacre is why people buy pearls, and they, in turn, are tied to the degree of transparency of the nacre. It is this transparency that allows people to look into the pearls. If some contaminant in the water causes the nacre to lose its fabled transparency, the pearl's value plunges.

- **The color of the pearls**—Pearls come in multiple colors with white, black, gray, silver, green, and gold being the most popular.
  - Far and away, white pearls are the most popular. White pearls are most valuable when they are bright white, as opposed to a creamy white, off-white, or eggshell. In addition to the pearl's primary color, most pearls have a secondary tint, with rose being the most popular. The two most popular white pearls come from:
    - › The Akoya oyster, which produces traditional pearls that range in size from 3mm to 10mm
    - › The White South Sea oyster which produces larger pearls (9mm and larger) that change appearance under different light and are highly valued
  - Pearls are heat-treated and bleached to brighten them. Since these changes are permanent, the treatments are allowable.
  - Black pearls (which are really dark gray) are produced by the black-lipped Black South Sea oyster, found off Tahiti

and Okinawa. These oysters also produce green, silver, and gray pearls depending upon where the irritant is placed in the oyster.

- Gold pearls are produced by the gold-lipped oyster. The color can range from light champagne to deep gold, with the deep gold being the most valuable.

- **The cleanliness of the pearl**—Cleanliness describes whether the surface is free of blemishes, cuts, discolorations, and the like. Blemish-free is best, of course, but small blemishes near the string hole are often not visible and don't severely reduce the value.

- **The shape of the pearl**—Pearls come in three shapes—spherical (round), symmetrical (oval), and baroque (free form). Spherical are the most valuable, all other factors being equal. Symmetrical pearls can make a pretty strand, provided they are matched—we'll talk more about matching pearls in a moment. Baroque pearls are irregularly shaped and should cost less.

- **The size of the pearl**—As with most gemstones, bigger is better. The price increases exponentially as the size increases arithmetically.

- **The match of the string**—Match refers to how well the pearls on the string complement each other. If they are the same color, tone, luster, then none of the pearls stand out as being better or worse than the others. It only takes one overly good (or bad) pearl to ruin a string's visual appeal.

The Advantage of Pearls

Unlike most fine jewels, pearls can be worn almost everywhere. They are appropriate at the office during the day, at a club at night, at the opera, or with a sweater at a football game.

The Disadvantages of Pearls

- The first disadvantage is that unlike emeralds and garnets, which are in limited supply, man can create an unlimited amount of pearls. Supply versus demand is always an issue over the long term.
- Pearls need to be restrung every 5 years if they are used frequently and every 10 years if they are used rarely. Over time, the string will dry out and become brittle.
- Perspiration and makeup stain pearls, so they need to be cleaned with a warm, damp cloth after they are worn.
- Pearls have a limited life. Unlike other jewels, which last forever, even with great care pearls will wear out within 100 to 150 years.

Warning Signs

When shopping for pearls:

- Look at the drill holes to see if a tint color was added with dye. If it was, there will be a tell-tale ring around the drill hole instead of the tint color being throughout the pearl.
- Each pearl should be tied individually so that if the string breaks only one pearl is at risk.
- The string should be pure, multifilament silk. Silk produces the strongest string if it is twisted properly.
- The recent tsunami in Japan may damage future pearl harvests. We might not know for years, and this is the pricing wild card.
- Pearls can be faked. The old "run them across your teeth and, if they are rough, they are real" test no longer works; Majorica brand fakes are also rough.

- Never buy pearls in China or from China; they are often of low quality and are mismarked.

The investment potential for pearls is very low. The return on investment from buying pearls comes from wearing them.

Author's personal note: Investors looking for a wide assortment of gemstones at great prices with exceptional service and advice should visit www.pioneergem.com. Run by Ed Nowak, Pioneer often has an inventory that exceeds 1,000 stones. Ed can be reached at (253) 833-1418.

JEWEL QUOTES

The pearl is the queen of gems and the gem of queens.

—AUTHOR UNKNOWN

Jewelry takes people's minds off your wrinkles.

—SONJA HENIE

These gems have life in them: Their colors speak, say what words fail of.

—GEORGE ELIOT

I have always felt a gift diamond shines so much better than one you buy for yourself.

—MAE WEST

There is in them a softer fire than the ruby, there is the brilliant purple of the amethyst, and the sea green of the emerald—all shining together in incredible union. Some by their splendor rival the colors of the painters, others the flame of burning sulfur or of fire quickened by oil.

—PLINY, ABOUT THE OPAL

I never worry about diets. The only carrots that interest me are the number you get in a diamond.

—MAE WEST

No gold-digging for me; I take diamonds! We may be off the gold standard someday.

—MAE WEST

This diamond has so many carats it's almost a turnip.

—RICHARD BURTON

I really think that American gentlemen are the best after all, because kissing your hand may make you feel very good but a diamond and a sapphire bracelet lasts forever.

—ANITA LOOS

The hues of the opal, the light of the diamond, are not to be seen if the eye is too near.

—RALPH WALDO EMERSON

The three rings of marriage are the engagement ring, the wedding ring, and the suffering.

—AUTHOR UNKNOWN

You can't cry on a diamond's shoulder, and diamonds won't keep you warm at night, but they're sure fun when the sun shines.

—ELIZABETH TAYLOR

My mother says I didn't open my eyes for eight days after I was born, but when I did, the first thing I saw was an engagement ring. I was hooked. I think men who have a pierced ear are better prepared for marriage. They've experienced pain and bought jewelry.

—RITA RUDNER

The rarest things in the world, next to a spirit of discernment, are diamonds and pearls.

—JEAN DE LA BRUYÈRE

When we long for life without difficulties, remind us that oaks grow strong in contrary winds and diamonds are made under pressure.

—PETER MARSHALL

Diamonds are a girl's best friend and a man's worst enemy.

—AUTHOR UNKNOWN

There are three things extremely hard: steel, a diamond, and to know one's self.

—BENJAMIN FRANKLIN

Will the people in the cheaper seats clap your hands? And the rest of you, if you'll just rattle your jewelry.

—JOHN LENNON

Perhaps time's definition of coal is the diamond.

—KAHLIL GIBRAN

All art is autobiographical; the pearl is the oyster's autobiography.

—FEDERICO FELLINI

CHAPTER TWELVE

Energy Exploration

No matter what happens with alternative energy sources, oil and gas are going to be the primary source of energy globally for the foreseeable future. There are thousands of ways to invest in oil and gas, including small oil stocks, global oil companies, oil futures, drilling service firms, platform manufacturers, oil service companies, energy ETFs, energy mutual funds, refiners, oil pipelines, pipe suppliers, drilling mud manufacturers, transportation companies, and the list goes on.

The problem with all of these traditional energy investment alternatives is that they have a highly positive correlation with the price of energy and the strength of the global economy. If the global economy is strong, the rest of the stock market will also be doing well and adding any of the above more traditional energy investments to a portfolio will not provide any significant improvement to a traditional portfolio of stocks and bonds.

However, the success of an energy exploration program is not correlated with:

- Other energy related investments
- The price of oil and gas
- The economy as a whole

Whether or not you find oil when you drill is unaffected by the level of the stock market or the current price of oil. It is impacted only by how much natural gas or oil is located where you happen to be drilling.

In a modern energy exploration partnership, there is a managing partner (often a corporation) that makes the day-to-day decisions regarding which:

- Energy rights to acquire and how much to pay for those rights
- Drilling contractor to use and to negotiate the deal with the contractor
- Gas pipeline or oil trucking company to use, and so forth

In short, the managing partner makes all the large and small decisions necessary to explore for energy.

Nonmanaging partners, who simply want to invest in order to save on taxes and generate cash flow, are referred to as general partners. In order to fully participate in the tax benefits, investors must be general as opposed to limited partners. General partners have unlimited liability related to the project, so investors should carefully review the project's insurance limits.

Energy exploration programs range from lower risk to very high risk. However, these names are often misnomers. In a typical low risk program, you pool your money (typically $30,000 to $300 million) with other accredited investors. Accredited investors have to confirm that they have one of the following:

- $1 million of investible funds (exclusive of home, car, and other personal collateral)
- An income that is greater than $300,000 for the last two years, with the expectation it will continue
- A trust that holds assets greater than $5 million

If the wells are drilled within the confines of an existing oil or gas field, into the same geologic formation, and producing wells are found to the north, east, west, and south, chances are these wells will also be producers. However, producing doesn't necessarily mean commercially viable.

As you might imagine, the cost of acquiring the mineral rights to a claim that is surrounded by successful commercial wells is very high. The partnership has to pay the landholder a large fee and/or a large royalty (20% to 40% of any energy produced). Next are all the costs for maintenance are paid. Of the remainder, the managing partner typically gets 10% for its services, leaving 50% to 70% of the remaining energy for the investors who put up the cash.

Natural Gas

Let's start with a natural gas drilling program. The money is usually paid into the program in stages. If you fail to remit the funds for each stage by the due date, you usually lose your entire interest. The first installment is used to drill the center holes for one to four new gas wells. A geologist then assesses the gas flow from each well to see if they are likely to be commercially viable. If any of the wells are not generating enough gas to be viable, their shafts are filled with cement. If they generate enough gas to suggest commercial viability, the next step is "fracking."

Fracking means that from the center hole, side shafts are drilled into the gas-bearing shale in two to six directions. These side tunnels can be up to 400 yards long. After the side holes are drilled, explosive charges are placed along the side tunnels at set intervals. Then the charges are simultaneously blown, fracturing the shale along the tunnel. Sand-infused water is pumped into the wells under high pressure. The sand gets between the layers of the shattered shale and holds them open to allow the gas to flow more freely. The water is then pumped out of the wells leaving the sand behind. Again, the wells are assessed for viability. Assuming the well is viable the "finish work" is done. This means placing concentration caps and regulators on top of the wells and getting them ready to hook into pipelines.

Some of the reasons why a low risk program may still have a lot of risk include:

- A roughneck could accidentally drop a wrench or hammer down the well hole—ruining the well.
- Sometimes fracking causes the well to flood with water from a previously unknown water table or underground pond—ruining the well. If the pump operator pumps out more water than was pumped in, there is a problem.
- Over the last few years, the price of natural gas has dropped sharply from $13.32 per 1,000 cubic feet (Mcf) to less than $1.89 per Mcf. A well which is hugely profitable at over $13 per Mcf can be a loser at less than $2 per Mcf.
- Even though gas is found, it can stop flowing after just a few months.
- The cost of acquiring drilling rights on "proven ground" can be so high that the investors might not get a positive return after paying the landowner and managing partner.

- Not all natural gas is equal. Some gas is weak gas and has a low BTU per thousand cubic feet of gas, while other natural gas is super gas. It is so concentrated that it can have three times the energy per 1,000 cubic feet as weak gas. Strong gas sells at a much higher price.
- Not all gas wells are conveniently located near a pipeline. The cost of connecting to a pipeline can be substantial if the nearest one is 10 or more miles away.
- These investments are illiquid. If you need to sell, you'll be lucky to receive $0.10 on the dollar.

Thus, finding energy is only half the risk of even a low risk program. Low risk programs are called such because the probability of finding energy is high. This does not mean the risk of loss is low.

At the other end of the spectrum are high risk programs like wildcat drilling for oil. In a wildcat program, you drill wells in an area where no oil has yet been found. In fact, you may be the first to even look for oil in a given area. As a result, acquiring the mineral rights is much cheaper (3% to 5% royalties). Allowing 10% for the managing partner, this means the investors receive 80% or more of any oil or gas. Usually in a wildcat program, if the first well(s) are successful, the original investors get the right to participate in additional programs in the same area on the same terms. This is a carrot to provide additional reward as compensation for the high level of risk. Estimates of success for pure wildcatting are hard to come by, but assuming a 1 out of 30 chance of success is probably reasonable. The success level rises as the amount and quality of the geologic work that precedes the decision to drill improves.

Not all oil wells are the same—nor is all oil. The oil that comes out of the ground varies from well to well based on the following factors:

- **Viscosity**—Light oil flows freely at room temperature, dark oil is more tar-like and must be heated to flow freely. Light oil is less expensive to transport and process and is therefore more valuable.
- **Sulfur level**—Sweet oil has a low level of contamination with sulfur. Sour oil is highly contaminated with sulfur. Sulfur is expensive to remove, so sweet oil is more valuable.
- **Other impurities**—Oil from each region has its own impurities that have to be refined out—the fewer impurities, the better.
- **Volume**—Forget the pictures you have seen of oil shooting hundreds of feet into the air. It is a very rare well that has enough natural pressure to self-pump oil to the surface. The typical well in the United States produces 10 barrels (420 gallons) of oil a day. A pump moves the oil from the base of the shaft to the surface where it is collected in a storage tank. A few times a week a truck comes by, empties the tank, and takes the oil to either a refinery or a collection point (barge, railhead) from which it is sent to a refinery. Without a refinery, oil is just sticky goo. Because oil is expensive to transport, oil becomes less valuable the further it is from a refinery.

The Tax Benefits

The tax benefits of drilling programs are substantial. All of the costs of acquiring, drilling, completing, and managing the well are tax deductible in the year they are incurred and are distributed to the investors on a pro-rata basis. Thus, if you invest $60,000 and the managing partner spends the entire $60,000, you get a $60,000 write-off. Assuming the investors are in the 40% tax bracket (federal and state) that write-off will save $24,000 in taxes.

In addition, the investor's income is also partially sheltered by the depletion deduction. This deduction lowers the capital value of an asset by the amount of minerals removed. For tax purposes, the depletion of minerals formula is:

> Depletion = (Units Produced / Total Units) × Cost
> (Costs / Value Lease) × (Costs − Previous Depletion)
> Suppose the partnership buys a mine site for $3MM that holds 100K ounces of palladium. In the first year it mines 40K ounces. The depletion deduction would be (40/100) × 3MM = 1.2MM.

Note that as of this writing the depletion deduction is being reviewed by both the White House and Congress—readers are encouraged to check for changes in the rules.

Selecting the Right Program

Finding a good energy program is not easy, and there are no sure things, but these guidelines should help eliminate most of the serious errors:

- Selecting a managing partner with a long consistent record of "hitting singles" is better than selecting one with a record consisting of the occasional home run followed by numerous dry holes. The more consistent the results, the more benefit there is to adding this alternative investment to a portfolio.
- The drilling program should have no relation to the marketing agent. There are thousands of drilling programs out there who want to raise capital to drill on a prospect they own or can lease. Independent firms that market these deals have their choice of which to represent. To enhance their own reputations, they will only market the programs they think

have the greatest chance for success. Therefore, they act as a free screening service.

- The managing partner should have a vast level of experience in energy exploration, a long record of delivering successful results for investors, and some bench depth so they are not dependent on the expertise of one person.
- The geologist or engineering firm should be independent of the managing partner so that all assessments and appraisals are at "arm's length."
- Make sure the managing partner has experience drilling the type of ground intended for drilling. Experience drilling gas shale is of little help if the program is looking for oil under a sheet of granite.
- States are becoming increasingly demanding on minimizing the environmental impact of drilling and requiring reclamation of dry hole sites. Make sure your program has adequate funds set aside to meet these requirements.
- Since every general partner has unlimited liability, it's essential to make sure the project has insurance that is sufficiently broad and deep to cover any contingency. Also, investors should check their own umbrella policies to see if they cover any spillover liability.

CHAPTER THIRTEEN

Real Estate

The classic argument for investing in real estate is: "They aren't making any more of the stuff." While there is a constant "supply" of real estate, the population is ever increasing—raising demand. Over time, this improves the demand/supply ratio that's so important from the investor's perspective. However, this argument is only true from one perspective.

Consider a large piece of beachfront property that has a single large house on it. While it is true that the lot is not going to get any larger, the owner of a single family home might sell it to a condo developer who puts up eight townhouse units on the same lot. Thus, eight families can now have beachfront homes where there use to just be one.

Carried to its logical conclusion, the single family home could be replaced with a 100-unit high-rise building. Now, there are 100 oceanfront homes where there was only one before. So, what's your definition of real estate? If it's the dirt, they are not making any more of it—at least not enough to matter. However, if your definition of real estate is oceanfront homes, higher density means that we are making more of the stuff. It is all in how you look at it.

Real estate investments come in two forms: equity and debt. Debt instruments are covered separately in my book *The Investor's Guidebook to Fixed Income Investments*, because they behave like other debt instruments. This chapter focuses on equity investments in real estate because they behave differently than traditional stocks and bonds—and thus are an alternative asset class.

TAXES AND REAL ESTATE

The government giveth and the government taketh away.

The government both provides tax benefits for real estate investors and imposes special taxes on real estate. The overall tax treatment can be a net positive or a net negative for the investor. The biggest advantage of investing in real estate is that real estate often appreciates in dollar terms, while at the same time, improvements are being depreciated for tax purposes—providing investors with a tax advantage. The easiest way to understand this advantage is through an example.

Suppose you buy a plot of land with a building on it for a total of $1 million. According to the tax assessor, the lot alone is worth $200K and the building on the lot (referred to as the improvement) is worth $800K. You put 20% down ($200K) and borrow the balance ($800K) with a 10-year, 6% interest-only mortgage. The monthly mortgage payment is $4K (($800K × .06%) / 12).

You sign a 10-year, triple net lease with a tenant with great credit quality at $70K per year. (The term "triple net" means that the tenant will pay the property taxes, insurance, utilities, and maintenance so that, even though you are the property's owner, you have no additional costs beyond the mortgage and administration of the lease.)

Your annual cash flow is $70K rent − $48K interest = $22K, which would normally be taxable income. However, under current tax law, you can depreciate the property's improvements over a 40 year life. The government allows for the depreciation of improvements because while the land itself lasts forever; buildings decay, rot, wear out, and eventually have to be replaced.

If you use straight line depreciation, that means $800K of improvements can be written off over 40 years. ($800K / 40 years = $20K per year.) This deduction shelters $20K of your $22K in annual income from taxes. Assuming overhead expenses of $2K per year generates an additional $2K a year in deductions, the taxable income to the property owner is now zero, even though the property is throwing the owner a net positive $20K in cash flow per year. While $20K a year only represents a 2% return on the $1 million property, it represents a 10% return on the $200K down payment—before factoring in any expected appreciation.

While depreciation lowers the current taxes, it also lowers the property's tax basis which increases taxes later on. For example, in 10 years, hopefully the property has appreciated and you can sell it for $1.5 million—net of all sales fees. The tax basis for the property is:

Purchase Price − Depreciation = Tax Basis
$1MM − $200K = $800K Tax Basis
The gain on sale is equal to the Sale Price − Tax Basis
$1.5MM − $800K = $700K Gain
Capital Gains tax at 20% ($700K × 20%) = $140K
So the net gain on sale is:
$1.5MM sales − $1MM purchase − $140K taxes = $360K

Thus, the cash flows (as shown in Figure 13.1) for 10 years on the $200K down payment invested are: $20K per year + $360K at the end of 10 years. The return on the original $200K investment is a healthy 14.11%.

FIGURE 13.1

Net Cash Flows for Above Investment

0	1	2	3	4	5	6	7	8	9	10
-$200K	$20K	$20K	$20K	$20K	$20K	$20K	$20K	$20K	$20K	$20K + $360K

While the depreciation deductions available under the federal tax code are a big plus in terms of taxes because they delay taxes and convert ordinary income into capital gains, the tax treatment for real estate is not all favorable. Although the federal government grants deductions to property investments, local governments are not so kind. Property is almost always subject to local property tax. This is odd because other investments are not. Stocks aren't subject to an annual stock tax. Bonds aren't subject to an annual bond tax. The local property tax is often substantial and reduces the investor's return. Michael Bloomberg, while mayor of New York, said not to raises taxes on what can move, referring to a tax on millionaires. Unfortunately for real estate investors, property can't be moved. This makes property taxes, property fees, and fines for the misuse or neglect of property an attractive source of revenue generation for politicians.

Some additional risks of real estate in general include:

- **Local overbuilding**—Whether it's office space, apartments, or hotels, overbuilding negatively impacts the rents of the other competitive buildings in the area. This naturally also reduces return.

- **Nearby construction**—No one wants to live or work next to a noisy construction site. Nearby construction temporarily reduces rents from both residential and commercial tenants. If the new building obstructs a great view or replaces a park, it can permanently reduce the projected rental income.

- **Changing building and/or occupancy codes**—Complying with ever-changing building codes and occupancy rules can be expensive, especially when compliance requires retrofitting older buildings.

- **Prior environmental contamination of the ground or building**—If a building or ground has any environmental contamination, the owners can be liable for the cleanup regardless of whether they had anything to do with creating the contamination. For example, if you buy an apartment building and it turns out that there is some old lead paint in a closet, you can be liable for the cleanup, as well as any neurological damages to children who ingest the paint. If you buy a tract of raw land in Florida and someone dumps toxic waste on your property, you are liable for all costs of the cleanup and all damages.

- **The tenant(s) go broke and cannot (or will not) pay their rent**—There is a limited supply of high credit quality tenants. Ironically, the usual offset for accepting lower credit quality tenants—charging more rent to offset the higher credit risk— just increases the probability of default.

- **The tenant(s) move out**—There is a limited supply of replacement tenants, as well. You may find yourself in a situation where replacement tenants:
  - Can't be found

- Can only be found after a long period when the property is unoccupied and generates no income
- Can only be found after reducing the rent or making costly improvements as an enticement
- **A decline in property value**—The property's value declines due to lack of maintenance or improper maintenance.
- **A local or national economic decline**—The property's in a region suffering from local economic decline or national economic decline.
- **Zoning codes**—The property is subject to zoning law changes that limit the property's potential and adversely affects its value.
- **Eminent domain**—The property may be subject to eminent domain before it is allowed to reach its full value.
- **Rising costs**—The property taxes, water and sewer fees, utility rates, and labor costs may rise at a faster rate than rents.

Real estate comes in many different forms—each of which has its own characteristics, advantages and disadvantages from an investor's perspective, and unique issues that investors need to consider. Let's look at some of the major categories of investment real estate.

Commercial Office Space

- The advantages of investing in commercial office space include:
  - Leases tend to be long term (up to 20 years) and so the space turns over less often—meaning that new tenants don't have to be constantly sourced.
  - Commercial property is rarely, if ever, subject to rent controls.

- The disadvantages of investing in office space include:
  - Tenants often require extensive "build-outs" or "build to suit." Build-outs include the walls, carpeting, crown molding, lighting, kitchens, lobby counters, and so forth that developers often must provide to entice clients. Build to suit means that the developer will build an entire building to suit the needs of a prospective tenant.
  - Long-term leases offer less opportunity to raise rents.
  - It is sometimes difficult to match available space with prospective tenants needs—it seems tenants always want more (or less) space than the developer has available.
  - Tenants often want a guaranteed option to expand. This requires the owner to inventory empty space "just in case" the tenant exercises the expansion option.
  - Increased use of "work from home" and "remote access" technology is reducing the need for office space.
- The main issue with office spaces is the optimization of rental income. Owners try to optimize rental income via an algorithm that uses the following inputs:
  - Number of tenants—There are two common strategies here:
    - Some buildings have a single tenant. If the tenant leaves the entire building has to be re-let. If the building can be re-let quickly, inexpensively, and at a higher rent, the turnover is a huge plus. If not, it's a huge risk.
    - Some purposely seek hundreds of small tenants to capture the lower risk and lower reward of "tenant diversity."
  - Credit quality of tenants—Some landlords only want premium credit tenants. Others will take lower quality tenants in exchange for higher rents and hope to still have a higher return after any missed rent payments and other expenses.

- Expected time to secure new tenants—If the economy is strong and vacancy rates are low, finding new tenants is usually easy.
- Required build-outs for new tenants—A landlord might pass on a tenant who requires far more expensive build-outs for another who wants to pay less rent, but requires less expense up front.
- Ability to raise rents—If the vacancy rate is expected to decrease, a landlord would push for a shorter lease with more opportunity to raise rent. If the vacancy rate is expected to increase, the landlord will opt for longer term leases.
- Staggered lease maturity—If the building has multiple tenants, do the leases all come due at the same time or are the maturities staggered? If they do at the same time, it is easier for tenants to increase or decrease the amount of space they take. If they are staggered, there is less risk of the entire building being empty.

- Differing levels of prestige—Commercial space is designated A, B, or C.
  - An "A" space is the most prestigious space in the city and is typically characterized by:
    - Prime locations near mass transit and parks
    - High credit quality tenants
    - Finish work done to high standards:
      - Few internal columns to allow for flexible open space declines
      - Floor to ceiling windows
      - Restaurants on site
      - Impressive lobby
      - Thick moldings and high-quality carpets
      - Indirect lighting

* State-of-the-art mechanicals (elevators/air condition-ing/water/heat)
- A "B" space is a full level below and is characterized by:
  > A quality, safe office space
  > Often includes older buildings that have "some charm"
  > Less-convenient locations
  > Lower quality clients
  > Smaller floorplans
  > Fewer amenities
- "C" properties are characterized as:
  > Providing utilitarian space
  > Worn out in appearance
  > Offering limited mechanicals, such as small elevators
  > Lacking separate freight elevators
  > Serviced by narrow hallways

- Developing office space—Some real estate partnerships go a step further and actually develop space instead of just buying and leasing it.
  - In some cities, it can take a decade just to get the necessary permissions to build a substantial office building. EPA studies; traffic studies; and approvals from local development boards, borough, and city councils may all be obstacles that must be overcome to obtain a building permit.
  - Often a development partnership will start by acquiring neighboring small tracts of land and/or adjacent small buildings that it hopes to combine into a larger parcel. This must be done discretely. If word gets out that a developer needs to acquire just one more small building to have the land needed to build a large one, the price of that building will soar. Often, dummy corporations and trusts are used to hide the true owner's identity.

- In some cities, the partnership also has to acquire "air rights" that allow it to grow above a certain height.
- Assuming all the approvals are obtained, the actual construction process is far more difficult in a city. The building may need to be built between existing buildings, sometimes with just a few feet of separation. This requires special care and workers with unique skill sets. Deliveries of materials to the job site may be limited to one truck at a time, thus requiring extensive planning and staging. Noise restrictions limit the number of hours per day that construction can proceed. All of these raise costs.
- Often city construction means using union labor which, while usually very competent, is very expensive and moves at its own pace.

Suburban Office Space

Suburban office space is characterized by buildings that are:

- Usually two to six stories in height
- Rented to professional firms (such as law, accounting, architecture, or brokerage) and regional sales offices of national firms
- Near highways, train access to nearest city, and the airport

Advantages include:

- Easier access to building permits, as towns want the property tax income
- Easier and cheaper construction than office space in the city

Disadvantages include:

- The buildings are interchangeable. Most suburban office parks are a commodity, which limits pricing power
- The ease of building results in frequent overbuilding

Issues:

- Does the business owner have numerous buildings in the same area? If so, it is easier to retain tenants. Tenants expand and contract quickly. Being able to accommodate their changing need for space is a key to long-term success.

Warehouse Space

Warehouse space is characterized by the following:

- Low-cost construction with a limited amount of finished floor space that is typically used as functional office space
- Large open storage space that can be configured to suit

The advantages of investing in warehouse space include:

- Inexpensive to build
- Easy to maintain

The disadvantages of investing in warehouse space include:

- Warehouse buildings are a commodity, with the exception of location.
- Warehouse space is often built to suit a single tenant. If that tenant leaves, it may be hard to find a replacement tenant that needs the same amount of space configured the same way.

Issues that should be considered when investing in warehouse space include:

- Location
  - Near highways, rail heads, docks, and population centers
  - Near customers
- Configuration/design issues
  - Column spacing—the further apart, the better
  - Floor height—the higher the better
  - Weight flooring can take—the higher the better
  - Number of trucking bays—the more, the better

Industrial Property

Industrial properties are characterized by having been built to suit a particular tenant, such as:

- An auto assembly plant
- A foundry
- A steel plant
- A semiconductor plant
- A sawmill
- A printing company

The advantages of investing in industrial properties include the following:

- Local governments often offer property tax and/or utility rate breaks for developers who build industrial spaces that house highly paid manufacturing jobs.
- Usually, there is not a lot of competition from other suitable space.

The disadvantages of investing in industrial spaces include:

- Often, the structures are built to the exact specs of a particular tenant.
- Industrial spaces are tough buildings to repurpose. It is difficult to transform an auto plant into a shopping mall.

Issues to be considered before investing in industrial spaces include:

- **Availability and price of water**—Some manufacturing processes require large quantities of water which might either be unavailable or too expensive.
- **Availability, price, and reliability of electricity**—Some manufacturing processes require very well regulated power.
- **Right to work**—Do employees have to join a union in order to work at a company?
- **Access to transportation facilities**—Is the property close to railroad spurs, major highway intersections, or a port?
- **Loading and unloading facilities**—How many bays and loading docks are available?

Retail Space

Retail space can be divided in three broad categories; stand-alone malls, anchored strip malls, and strip malls. A typical investment structure looks like the one shown in Figure 13.2. An investor, or group of investors, raises capital and buys or builds some retail space. The group may or may not leverage its equity by taking on a mortgage. The partnership then either leases the entire mall to a mall operating company or hires a mall operating company to run the business. The mall operator then solicits stores and manages the mall.

FIGURE 13.2

Retail Space Investment Structure

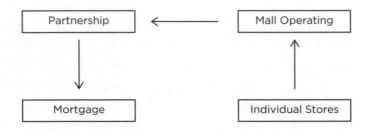

- Stand-alone malls are large collections of 50 to 400 or more stores usually anchored by three or more large department stores. They are located in highly populated areas usually where highways intersect. Examples of stand-alone malls include:
  - The Short Hills Mall in Short Hills, New Jersey, has Nordstrom, Neiman Marcus, Saks Fifth Avenue, Bloomingdale's, and Macy's as anchor stores.
  - The Galleria in Houston, Texas, has Neiman Marcus, Saks Fifth Avenue, and Macy's as anchor stores.
  - The Mall of America in Bloomington, Minnesota, has Nordstrom, Sears, and Macy's as anchor stores.
  - The King of Prussia Mall in King of Prussia, Pennsylvania, includes Macy's, Nordstrom, Bloomingdale's, Lord & Taylor, Neiman Marcus, Sears, and JCPenney as anchor stores.
- Anchored strip malls have one or two large stores which drive traffic to the mall. The anchor stores can be a Walmart, Bed

Bath & Beyond, Cabela's Sporting Goods, CVS, Walgreens, or a large food store. The mall will have another 5 to 30 stores, typically including a pet store, an auto parts store, a liquor and wine store, shoe stores, packaging stores, bookstores, a Radio Shack, a bowling alley, restaurants, and the like.

- Last are unanchored strip malls that contain stores of local interest, such as a dry cleaner, a Laundromat, a pizza parlor, an ice cream parlor, a sandwich shop, a newsstand, a barber shop, a nail salon, a beauty parlor, a Chinese take-out restaurant, a bagel shop, and so forth.

The advantages of investing in retail space include:

- Construction and maintenance are relatively simple.
- The deal can be structured anywhere along the risk spectrum from low risk/low reward to high risk/high reward. In a low risk-reward deal, the management company pays a flat fee to rent the mall. In a high risk-reward deal, the management company pays a low base rent plus a percentage of sales. In this case, the partnership's return is tied to the success of the stores in the mall. Retailers usually prefer the low rent/share of sales formula since it lowers their breakeven and transfers some of the business risk to the mall owners.

The disadvantages of investing in retail space include:

- The switch to internet shopping has reduced floor traffic dramatically—a trend that will continue.
- Many shoppers go to stores just to see the merchandise—and then go online to order it at a lower price—or use the online price to negotiate a lower price.

- As the population ages, it shops less. For teenagers, shopping is almost *the* national pastime. As a result of aging, estimates are that we have an excess of 20% to 25% of retail space.
- Retail space is not easy space to repurpose. Some malls have been transformed into charter schools or art galleries, but it is not easy.
- Shopping malls require large amounts of unproductive land for parking.
- Retail tenants regularly default on leases or want to renegotiate leases after they are signed. As the landlord, mall owners have to decide whether it is better to reduce the rent or have empty space.

Residential Rentals

Apartments generally come in three types:

- High-rise buildings range from the ultra-luxurious to ones that would be described as barely utilitarian. The luxurious buildings offer amenities such as underground parking, spas, gyms, pools, dog walks, gardens, state-of-the-art security systems, and doormen. The apartments themselves offer huge designer kitchens, spa baths, floor-to-ceiling windows, fireplaces, balconies, rich paneling, crown moldings, and hardwood flooring. The utilitarian apartments offer none of the above.
- Garden complexes are usually located in the suburbs and are two to three story units that appeal to young families and empty nesters.
- Small buildings (typically 2- to 10-unit single buildings) can be located in the city, suburbs, or small towns.

The advantages of investing in residential properties include:

- The leases are usually short (1 to 3 years) and provide opportunities to periodically raise rates.
- The high diversity of tenants minimizes the credit exposure to each individual tenant.

The disadvantages include:

- Residential complexes represent the easiest type of business when it comes to getting permits to build. This often results in overbuilding.
- Apartments require a high level of maintenance, as appliances break down. Many jurisdictions require the apartment be painted and re-carpeted every time a new tenant moves in to the apartment.
- Apartments are a commodity. With few exceptions, most of the apartments in the same area and price range are equally attractive.
- In some jurisdictions, rent control limits the value of leases. There are always more tenants than landlords, and politicians will always buy the votes of the majority with the wealth of the minority. If there is a shortage of apartments and rents rise sharply, rent control may follow.

Consider these issues before investing in residential properties:

- The key to apartment rents is vacancy levels. When vacancy levels fall below 4%, rents rise. When vacancy levels exceed 10%, rents fall. In between, rents are fairly steady—adjusted by 1% to 3% for inflation.

- A flood of short sales and foreclosures can create a wave of inexpensive housing rentals that will compete against apartments.

Hotel Programs

In a hotel partnership, the partners buy or build a building suitable to be used as a hotel and then enter into a contract with a hotel management company, such as Hilton, Marriott, Sheraton, or Red Roof Inn, to manage the hotel.

Characteristics of Hotels
Hotels fall into a few categories:

- **Destination Hotels**—These are hotels that people want to visit in and of themselves. These hotels offer numerous amenities, such as spas, beaches, pools, casinos, golf courses, and restaurants. Some examples of destination hotels are:
  - The Wynn, Aria, and Cosmopolitan in Las Vegas, Nevada
  - The Revel in Atlantic City, New Jersey
  - The Atlantis in the Bahamas
  - The Phoenix in Phoenix, Arizona
- **Transient Business Hotels**—These hotels are located in large cities and try to attract the business traveler on an expense account and, more importantly, the "business meeting" business. These hotels generally have large and small conference rooms that offer companies space for meetings for prospects, customers, or their own staff. These meetings not only generate room rentals, but also audio-visual rentals, catering income, and more. The market for transient business is divided into three groups:
  - *Luxury*—On the high end, you will find some of the Ritz-

Carlton and Four Seasons properties, the Fairmont in San Francisco, Palmer House in Chicago, and the Waldorf Astoria New York.

- *Moderate*—These properties include the downtown Hiltons, Sheratons, and Marriotts.
- *Budget*—In this category, you find Days Inn, Quality Inn, Hilton Garden Inn, and similar properties.

- **Transient Hotels**—Along every highway (especially at highway intersections) are hotels that cater to travelers. These motels offer a minimum of services—perhaps a pool, but typically no restaurant, no meeting rooms, or other amenities. Chain restaurants usually locate next door or nearby. Management companies include Holiday Inn, Red Roof Inn, and Quality Inn.
- **Extended Stay Hotels**—These properties are designed for stays of seven days to six months and include a small living room, kitchenette, bathroom, and bedroom. Many offer breakfast and happy hour. Examples include Embassy Suites, Homestead Suites, and Residence Inns.

Advantages of Hotels as Investments

The advantages of hotels as investment properties include:

- If you can rent a typical hotel room's 600 feet of space for $200 a night, every night, you gross $6,000 a month, $72,000 a year, or $1,440,000 over 20 years—enough to buy a McMansion. Thus, if you can consistently rent the room, the return on investment can be exceptional.
- Gift shops, restaurants, local parking, and such can also contribute substantially to the hotel's profitability.
- Hotel partnerships can be designed to be low risk, high risk, or any risk level in between. The partnership can be paid:

- A set fee for the use of the building (low risk)
- A lower set fee plus a fee for each room rented (moderate risk)
- No guaranteed fee at all, simply a split on all revenue (high risk)

Disadvantages of Hotels as Investments

The disadvantages of hotel properties as investments include:

- The rooms have to be resold every night—they are a wasting asset during the day.
- The travel services, such as Expedia, Hotwire, and Orbitz, now allow travelers to compare rates and have dramatically increased price competition.
- Politicians love to tax visitors since they don't vote. The revenue generated by some types of properties is subject to local taxes in addition to the property tax. For example, in New York City, hotel revenue is subject to the following taxes:
  - New York state tax (4%)
  - New York City tax (4.875%)
  - Hotel tax ($2 + 5.75%)
  - A convention fee ($1.50)
- Likewise, parking (hotels for cars) revenue in New York City is subject to an 18.375% tax. While these fees are paid by the visitor, they still hold down what the hotel or parking lot owner can charge for rooms or parking spots.
- Partners have to be careful when the management company has numerous hotels in the same area because the hotel management company controls the reservation system. Suppose a hotel chain has two deals with two different partnerships on two hotels near Disney World. On one hotel, it pays the part-

ners a flat fee per month regardless of occupancy level. Once that hotel reaches an occupancy level that covers the monthly fee, the hotel company receives 100% of the revenue. On the second hotel, the management company has 60/40 split with the owner partnership. In this case, the hotel management company has an incentive to steer "call in" traffic to the first hotel. By keeping the first hotel full, they leverage their fixed fee arrangement.

Raw Land

No real estate investment discussion would be complete without mentioning investments in raw (unimproved) land. There are three primary reasons to add raw land:

- The land may contain minerals.
- The land may contain aboveground or belowground water.
- The land is in the path of future development.

The big advantage of buying raw land is that it is relatively inexpensive to buy large tracts.

The big disadvantages of buying raw land include:

- Raw land doesn't generate any tax deductions.
- It generates negative cash flow. Raw land usually doesn't generate any income, but it is still subject to property tax.
- This type of investment exposes the owner to environmental risk. In many jurisdictions, Florida for example, the landowner is liable for any environmental damage—even if the landowner is remote. If a New York resident buys a tract of land in Florida, and a Florida local dumps toxic waste on the

land, the landowner is liable for all damage and cleanup costs. For this reason, it is essential to have adequate insurance and hold title to the land in a third-party corporate entity or trust.

Depending on where the land is located and its size, some raw land partnerships try to generate some income to at least offset the taxes by running a business that's easy to start and operate on the land. Some examples include:

- Short-term or long-term parking lots
- Miniature golf courses
- Golf driving ranges
- Host swap meets
- Shooting ranges
- Self-storage facilities
- Offering camping, fishing, hunting rights

Being able to bring in some income from raw land makes it much easier to be patient.

Specialty Housing

Assisted living and nursing homes represent perhaps the greatest current opportunity in real estate. This is one area of real estate that benefits from the aging of America. As the population ages, there will be greater and greater need for assisted living and nursing home facilities. As with hotels, the real estate company builds the facility and leases it to a management firm that operates the facility.

Primary Residences and Vacation Homes

While most people think of their home as their biggest investment—it is their biggest expense—a primary residence is definitely not an investment. Between taxes, mortgage interest, maintenance, insurance, utilities, and the like, it's questionable whether owning or renting is a more cost-effective housing solution. While the answer to the "rent vs. buy" decision probably varies from market to market, a primary residence should not be part of the investor's portfolio pie chart.

Farmland

Farmland has become one of the most popular alternative investments. Let's first look at the advantages and disadvantages of investing in farmland, the major types of farmland, and then at the different ways to invest.

The biggest advantages of farmland investments are that:

- **People have to eat frequently**—While hydroponics has made great strides, it takes land to grow most crops.
- **The world's population is growing**—Each year more food is required to sustain it.
- **As people become wealthier, they consume more meat**—As meat consumption increases, the demand for cereals to feed the animals explodes. The increasing wealth of China is responsible for a 4% annual increase in cereal consumption that is unrelated to population growth.
- **Farmland is disappearing around the world**—Farmland is disappearing because of suburban expansion, loss due to erosion, loss due to depletion, and loss due to environmental contamination and environmental restrictions.

- **Rising crop prices**—As the western countries resort to printing currency to pay their food bills, inflation and hyperinflation become inevitable.
- **Federal price supports**—The federal government pays farmers not to plant when there is a surplus of a crop.
- **Federal Farm Credit Bank**—By accessing lines of credit at the FFCB, farmers can finance tractors, combines, and land purchases at well below market rates.
- **Improved seeds**—Genetically engineered seeds automatically fix nitrogen and are impervious to Roundup (a herbicide). These seeds eliminate the need to fertilize and weed fields.
- **Ability to buy insurance against most farm risks**—A well-evolved insurance market now allows farmers to insure their crop against almost every farm risk, including drought, flood, hail, wind, excessive heat, excessive cold, and pests. Note that the insurance may eliminate a loss, but usually not guarantee a profit.
- **Favorable tax treatment**—Farmland is taxed at a much lower property tax rate than other land uses.
- **Growing markets in biofuel**—More crops, particularly corn, are being diverted from food to biofuel production.
- **Healthier**—There is a growing, although embryonic, trend toward healthier eating, which places more emphasis on fresh fruits and vegetables.
- **Estate tax**—The way the estate tax in the United States is written makes it very difficult for family farms to stay in the family. If a farm has $10 million worth of land, the estate tax as of this writing would be $2.75 million. This tax forces many family farmers to sell to developers and reduces the available farmland.

The biggest disadvantages of farmland as an investment are:

- **Weather**—The return is dependent on the weather, which is unpredictable.
- **Politics**—Politics plays a huge role in the success of any farming venture. Government policies regarding exports, import barriers, railroad rate regulation, price supports, credit extensions, environmental regulations, and the like all mean that there is a high level of government involvement in the business.
- **Increased productivity**—Farm productivity is increasing and offsetting the decline in available farmland.
- **Soil depletion and erosion**—Soil becomes depleted over time and needs to be recharged. Erosion is also an ongoing problem than has to be carefully managed.
- **Diseases and pests**—New variations of diseases and pests are always emerging in an ongoing battle between farmers and pests.
- **Vegetarians**—The increase in the number vegetarians in the United States is offsetting the increase in meat eaters in other countries.
- **Single crop optimization**—Because of soil composition, pH, altitude, moisture content, average temperature, temperature range, duration of growing season, and similar factors, most farmland is optimized to produce one type of crop. Good soybean regions are too cool for corn. Good tomato regions are too acidic for potatoes. So, when an investor buys farmland, the investor's success or failure is usually tied to the price of a specific crop.

The price of a crop is driven by the following formula:

Starting inventory of crop in storage + (hectares planted × production per hectare) – consumption of the crop by all sources of consumption

With the exception of the starting inventory, the other three factors have numerous variables that determine their values.

Farmland is divided into five broad categories: grains, soybeans, orchards, landscaping and sod farms, and Christmas tree farms.

Grains

WHEAT

- Annual production is 700 million tons
- Is the third most commonly produced grain after corn and rice
- Two main types of wheat:
  - Common wheat
    - ❯ Started as a grass in the fertile crescent
    - ❯ Plant in the spring—harvest in the fall
    - ❯ Varieties and uses:
      - ✳ Durum wheat—makes semolina flour for pasta
      - ✳ Hard red spring—bread
      - ✳ Hard white—brewing
      - ✳ Soft white—pastries
  - Winter wheat
    - ❯ Plant in the fall, hardens over the winter, harvest in the spring
    - ❯ The main variety is hard red winter, which is used for bread

CORN

- Annual production is 785 million tons
- Corn is used in thousands of:

- Food products: oil, corn flakes, polenta, tamales, etc.
- Non-food products, degradable plastic, disposable diapers, explosives, soap, aspirin—and most importantly, Kentucky Bourbon
  - America has the most productive corn-growing regions (>2.5 tons per acre)

Soybeans

- Miracle plant has nitrogen-fixing capability
- Replenishes the soil
- One of the five sacred plants in China
- Referred to in Japan as "tuna of the mountains"
- Beans mature in 80 to 120 days
- Uses:
  - Food products: tofu, soysauce, tempeh, bean paste, etc.
  - Added to hundreds of products as soybean oil
  - Non-food products; adhesive, textiles (azlon), paint, polish, pens, waxes

Orchards

The major fruits include apples, oranges, lemons, and cherries.

- Benefit from trend to healthier diets
- Fruit trees tend to be very fragile. For example, if an orange tree is exposed to freezing temperatures, it can take 5 years to recover

Landscaping and Sod Farms

Including trees, shrubbery, and other decorative plants. The success of these programs depends on the strength of the new housing market. New homes require substantial landscaping.

Christmas Tree Farms

Advantages inclue:

- Requires a minimum of work—Clear-cut a field at the right altitude. Buy very small trees from a nursery (6 inches to 12 inches in height) and plant them on a 5-foot grid. Twice a year mow the area between the trees until they reach 4 feet in height and their shadow alone kills the underbrush. Trim the trees twice a year to optimize the shape. Harvest them when they reach 6 to 8 feet.
- The trees can be sold remotely, either wholesale or retail. As the holidays approach, independent truckers buy truckloads of trees and then resell them to local merchants in their home markets. Operators can also place ads on the internet and specialty catalogs, where people go to order the tree they want and have it shipped to them—guaranteed to arrive fresh. Operators can also enter into contracts with fund-raising groups, such as church and school groups. The fund-raising groups then sell a truckload of trees locally in their markets.

Disadvantages include:

- The main disadvantage to the business of growing natural Christmas trees is artificial trees. Every time a family buys an artificial tree, it reduces the size of the market for natural trees. Artificial trees sales have risen because:
  - The artificial trees are becoming much better looking— fuller and more natural.
  - As the population gets older, fewer families have small children, who are the biggest proponents of live trees.

- More stringent environmental regulations make disposal of the trees more difficult. Years ago, in many small towns, the dead dried trees were collected after the first of the year and the town had a late evening tree burning which marked the end of the holiday season. Today, the EPA prohibits tree burning in many locations.

Structuring Farmland Programs

Farmland programs can be structured in a variety of ways, including:

- **Buy the land and rent it for cash**—This first alternative is the most conservative. After buying the land, the partnership leases it to an operating company or farmer for a growing season, a set period of time, like 5 years, or a set period with an option to renew. In this case, the farmer takes 100% of the farming risk. The only risks to the program are incurred if the farmer goes bankrupt and can't pay the rent or is a poor steward of the land and damages it through erosion or depletion.
- **Buy land and trade it for share of the crop**—In this case, the partnership and the farmer share the farming risk and reward.
- **Buy land and hire operators to farm it**—The operators are paid in cash by the hour or by the season. The partnership takes 100% of the farming risk.

Thus, these programs range from low risk/low reward to high risk/high reward. They can be highly focused on one crop in one region or diversified across different states, different crops, and different deal structures. There is something for everyone.

Timberland

Many countries have deforested whatever forests they had centuries or decades ago. The remaining forest land globally is fewer than 980 million hectares (a little fewer than 2.5 billion acres) and is concentrated in the following regions:

- Russia
- Brazil
- Canada and the United States
- China

A typical timberland partnership is divided into three stages:

1. Acquiring timberland and/or harvesting rights for a certain time period

   As with any investment, investors want to buy when prices are low and sell when high. The trough of a global recession is the ideal time to buy since there is little demand for lumber and timberland is cheap.

   Some programs focus on the softwoods (pine) for paper production. This crop grows very quickly but is not very valuable "per tree." Other programs focus on the slower growing, but more valuable, hardwoods that are used for furniture.

   Some partnerships just want the lumber and elect to just secure the harvesting rights to a certain number of trees over a limited term (10 to 20 years). Other programs buy the land making two bets; that lumber will rise and so will the price of the timberland. The depletion rights go to the owner of the land—not the harvester.

   Some partnerships are highly geographically concentrated or

only focus on a single species of tree to harvest. Other programs intentionally diversify both locations and species. The diversified programs have less risk—but are more expensive to operate.

As always, logistics play a key role. It is sometimes better to buy a more expensive tract of land that is closer to a mill than a cheaper one that is further away.

2. Managing the land

The programs that actually purchase the timberland must pay property tax. In order to avoid negative cash flow when they are not harvesting trees, the program can sell camping rights, hunting rights, fishing rights, water rights, and the like.

Part of managing the timberland is yield optimization over the long term. Variables include:

The ratio of "clear cutting" to "selective harvesting." Clear cutting results in more lumber revenue today—but reduces the resale value of the land. Selective harvesting reduces revenue today (and raises costs) but, if done properly, can cause the value of the land to rise significantly.

The cost of putting in access roads and bridges versus using helicopters to fly the logs out.

The decision of whether to harvest today—or let the trees continue to grow. The value of a tree rises exponentially as its diameter increases arithmetically. A 20-inch diameter tree is worth twice as much as a 16-inch diameter tree because the tree can generate wider boards.

These decisions require the services of a very experienced lumber executive. As with all partnerships, the skills of the managing partner are the key to success.

3. Disposal phase

If the land was selectively harvested it can be sold to:

Another timber program for those programs that buy the land and clear cut. After the timber has been harvested, the value of the land drops until the trees have time to grow back. This usually takes 20 to 30 years. The program may hold the land to create carbon credits to offset other sources of pollution until it is time to harvest again. Unlike oil and copper, timber is a renewable resource.

Most programs don't want to wait that long. These programs will sell the land to:

Another timber program or paper company with a longer horizon

Conservationists who will turn the land into a wild habitat reserve

The federal, state, or county government for use as parkland or wild habitat reserve

Timber programs have a unique set of risks that don't impact other investments. These include the following:

- Various insects and diseases can wreak havoc on forests. According to the US forest service, there are more than 70 insects and more than 27 diseases that can destroy entire hectares of forest—typically by defoliation.
- While fires are sometimes necessary to strengthen a forest, a bad fire will set growth back by 40 years and wipe out lumber investors. It is almost impossible to obtain fire insurance for raw timberland at a reasonable cost.
- As the price of lumber rises, so does the theft of logs. Small thefts are carried out by local people who use the logs to heat

their homes or for building furniture. Large-scale thefts occur when a rogue group of axmen steal an entire stand of timber. If they are caught, they simply say they read the map wrong and pay for damages. Trees don't have ID numbers, so the mill has no way of knowing that the logs are stolen. Trees are hard to protect, especially when they are spread over thousands of acres.

- Drought will bring growth to a halt. Trees may survive a drought, but they don't grow much. Investors who are counting on growth may have their return delayed by years.
- Environmental legislation can impact programs. An ever increasing number of environmental regulations restrict what loggers can do, even on their own property.

The investment outlook for timber is exceptional. The growing middle class in the BRICs will consume more wood per person and the size of forest land continues to decline.

Ways to Invest in Real Estate

There are three primary ways to invest in real estate: directly, through a LLC or Sub-S, or through real estate investment trusts.

Investing "directly" means you buy the real estate, either in your own name or as a general partner in a partnership with others. The problems with buying directly is you have unlimited liability and limited liquidity. Suppose you buy a strip mall in your own name and fail to promptly remove snow from the parking lot. As a result, a school bus has an accident and numerous children are seriously hurt. You can be held liable, and all of your assets are at risk if any judgments are lodged against you.

Therefore, it is far more common for an investor to invest indirectly through an LLC or Sub-S in which the investor has total or at least a controlling interest. The reason for buying the real estate through a limited liability corporation or subchapter S corporation is to limit your liability. If the property is owned by an LLC or Sub-S, only the company assets—the property itself—is at risk. If your insurance doesn't cover the losses, you might lose the property, but not your other assets. The disadvantage of this form of ownership is that the investment is still relatively illiquid.

The third way to buy real estate is through a real estate investment trust (REIT). REITs are basically mutual funds that invest in real estate. They can be private or public but must have at least 100 owners. Like mutual funds, they have to pay out 90% of their taxable income in the year in which it is received to avoid double taxation. They need to receive at least 75% of their income from rents or mortgage interest. Most, but not all, REITs specialize in a particular type of real estate. Figure 13.3 lists several examples.

FIGURE 13.3

Some Popular REITs and Their Specialties

Symbol	Name	Type of Real Estate
VNO	Vornado	Diversified
BRE	BRE Properties	High-end apartment buildings
DCT	DCT Industrial Trust	Industrial properties
RSE	Rouse Properties	Regional malls
AKR	Acadia Realty Trust	Shopping centers
BXP	Boston Properties	Office towers
PCL	Plum Creek	Timber
LTC	LTC Properties	Health care
ACC	American Campus	Student dormitories

REAL ESTATE QUOTES

Ninety percent of all millionaires become so through owning real estate.

—ANDREW CARNEGIE

The major fortunes in America have been made in land.

—JOHN D. ROCKEFELLER

The best investment on earth is earth.

—LOUIS GLICKMAN

Landlords grow rich in their sleep.

—JOHN MILL

Land increases more rapidly in value at the centers and about the circumference of cities.

—WILLIAM E. HARMON

Every person who invests in well-selected real estate in a growing section of a prosperous community adopts the surest and safest method of becoming independent, for real estate is the basis of wealth.

—THEODORE ROOSEVELT

Land monopoly is not only monopoly, but it is by far the greatest of monopolies; it is a perpetual monopoly, and it is the mother of all other forms of monopoly.

—WINSTON CHURCHILL

If history could teach us anything it would be that private property is inextricably linked with civilization.

—AYN RAND

Just as man can't exist without his body, so no rights can exist without the right to translate one's rights into reality, to think, to work and keep the results, which means: the right of property.

—AYN RAND

The earth is the general and equal possession of all humanity and therefore cannot be the property of individuals.

—LEO TOLSTOY

The slogan of the National Association of Landlords is the comma-less "We Shelter You America." The truth of the matter is, however, that landlords shelter no one, while in fact the law shelters them . . . from the immediate expropriation that would occur if there were not force of gun and jail to back up this phoney, abusive, so-called property right.

—FRED WOODWORTH

I bought a two story property—it had one story before I bought it, and another story after.

—AUTHOR UNKNOWN

If you think no one cares about you—miss a few mortgage payments.

—AUTHOR UNKNOWN

The newest financial innovation is the "temporary mortgage"—it lasts only until the foreclosure.

—AUTHOR UNKNOWN

The dream of the last generation was to pay off their mortgage—the dream of the new generation is to get one.

—AUTHOR UNKNOWN

Only in America can you borrow money for the down payment, take out a first and second mortgage, add a home equity loan—and still call yourself a homeowner.

—AUTHOR UNKNOWN

One of the benefits of alternative investments is that they have a low correlation with traditional stocks and bonds and therefore improve the return/risk portfolios when they are added to traditional portfolios. This last advantage is the key to modern portfolio management. Correlation measures the degree to which two assets behave similarly. The scale runs from –1 (perfectly negative) to +1 (perfectly positive).

For example, the chart in Figure A.1 illustrates two asset classes that exhibit perfectly positive correlation. When asset one doubles in value, so does asset two. The portfolio's value is the sum of the two asset classes, and while the portfolio goes from $15.00 to $27.50 over 6 years, the investor's ride between the starting value and ending value is very volatile. Volatility creates too many opportunities for irrational exuberance and suicidal depression.

FIGURE A.1

Perfectly Positive Correlation

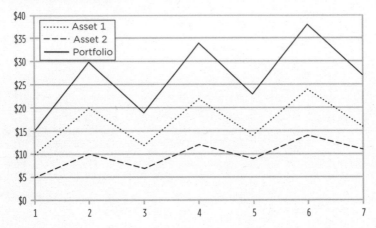

On the other hand, the two asset classes shown in Figure A.2 have a perfectly negative correlation. This means that when the value of one asset class increases, the value of the other decreases. As before, the portfolio's value is the sum of the two assets—but in this case the portfolio's value rises evenly over time with little volatility.

Perfectly Negative Correlation

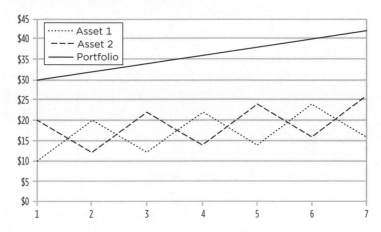

As an example, let's first look at a portfolio composed of just stocks and bonds and assume the data shown in Figure A.3. (Note that risk is measured as the standard deviation of the annual return for the asset class.) Figure A.4 shows the formula for calculating the return.

Table of Asset Class Data

Historic reward, risk, and correlation of two asset classes.

	Return	Risk
Equities	10%	25%
Fixed Income	4%	10%
Correlation	85%	

The formula for the return of a two asset class portfolio is a simple weighted average, as shown in Figure A.4.

FIGURE A.4

Formula for Calculating the Return of a Two Asset Class Portfolio

$$\text{Return} = W_1 R_1 + W_2 R_2$$

For example, a 50%-50% portfolio of the asset classes described in Figure A.3 would offer a return equal to the weighted average returns of the individual classes, as follows:

$$\text{Return} = (50\% \times 10\%) + (50\% \times 4\%) = 7\%$$

The formula for the risk of a two asset class portfolio is a little more complicated than the weighted average, because the correlation of the asset classes must be taken into account, as shown in Figure A.5.

FIGURE A.5

Formula for Calculating the Risk of a Two Asset Class Portfolio

$$\text{Risk} = \sigma = \sqrt{W_1^2 \sigma_1^2 + W_2^2 \sigma_2^2 + 2W_1 W_2 \sigma_1 \sigma_2 r_{12}}$$

$$\text{Risk} = \sigma = \sqrt{(.5^2 \times .25^2) + (.5^2 \times .1^2) + (2 \times .5 \times .5 \times .25 \times .1 \times .85)} = 16.96\%$$

If the correlation was +1, the risk would also be a simple weighted average—a 50/50 average.

$$(25\% + 10\%) / 2 = 17.5\%$$

However, since the correlation is less than +1, so is the risk level. A correlation of +.85 reduces the risk from 17.5% to 16.96%, as shown in Figure A.6.

FIGURE A.6

Impact of Correlation on Risk of the Portfolio Described in Figure A.3

Correlation	Risk
1.00	17.50%
0.85	16.96%
0.70	16.39%
0.55	15.81%
0.40	15.21%
0.25	14.58%
0.10	13.92%
0	13.46%
−0.10	12.99%
−0.25	12.25%
−0.40	11.46%
−0.55	10.61%
−0.70	9.68%
−0.85	8.66%
−1.00	7.50%

Clearly the lower the correlation between stocks and bonds, the lower the risk level of the portfolio.

There are, however, four issues:

- Stocks and bonds tend to have a high correlation, so they do little to hedge each other's risk. When one declines so does the other.
- The correlation has some volatility over the short term. The +.85 in this example is the "average" correlation over the long term. It fluctuates based on what else is going on in the

market. There are times when stocks and bonds move in unison (when investors put money in or pull money out of the market) and times when money moves back and forth between the asset classes. For example, lately there have been a number of "risk off, risk on" cycles. In these cycles, when stocks decline, bonds rise, and vice versa. These movements lower the correlation.

- The correlation goes through long-term drifts as the market environment changes. Thirty years ago the correlation between stocks and bonds was in the high +.60s. The long-term drift has been toward a higher correlation.
- In a market crash, the correlation of stocks and bonds approaches "1." However, just because both stocks and bonds may decline together, doesn't mean they will rise together. Either may rise well before the other.

Now let's add an allocation to an alternative asset class that has a negative correlation with traditional stocks and bonds. Figure A.7 lists the characteristics and Figure A.8 shows the formula for calculating the return on the multi-asset class portfolio.

FIGURE A.7

Data for a Three Asset Class Portfolio

	Weighting	Return	Risk
Equities	60%	10%	25%
Fixed Income	20%	6%	10%
Alternative Asset	20%	8%	15%
Correlations	Class 1-2 + .85		
	Class 1-3 − .10		
	Class 2-3 − .15		

FIGURE A.8

Formula for Calculating the Return of a Multi-Asset Class Portfolio

$$\text{Return} = W_1R_1 + W_2R_2 + \ldots + W_nR_n$$

For example, the return of a 60%–20%–20% portfolio of these asset classes would equal the weighted average return of the individual asset classes:

$$\text{Return} = (60\% \times 10\%) + (20\% \times 4\%) + (20\% \times 6\%) = 8\%$$

The formula for calculating the risk of a multi-asset class portfolio must take into account the correlation of each asset class with every other asset class, as shown in Figure A.9.

FIGURE A.9

Formula for Calculating the Risk of a Multi-Asset Class Portfolio

$$\text{Risk} = \sigma = \sqrt{([W_1]^2 [\sigma_1]^2 + [W_2]^2 [\sigma_2]^2 + \ldots + [W_n]^2 [\sigma_n]^2 + \Sigma_1^n (2W_1W_2\sigma_1\sigma_{2r}))}$$

$$\text{Risk} = \sigma = \sqrt{(.6^2 \times .25^2) + (.2^2 \times .1^2) + (.2^2 \times .15^2) + \sum \begin{array}{l} 2 \times .6 \times .2 \times .25 \times .10 \times .85 \\ 2 \times .6 \times .2 \times .25 \times .15 \times -.10 \\ 2 \times .2 \times .2 \times .10 \times .15 \times -.15 \end{array}} = 16.70\%$$

By adding the alternative asset class to the portfolio, an investor can increase the portfolio's return while also reducing its risk. The added return comes from increasing the allocation to the highest yielding asset class—equities. The lower risk results from the low correlation of the alternative asset class with traditional asset classes. Adding alternative asset classes to portfolios is becoming increasingly important as the correlation between traditional stocks and bonds becomes more positive.

information is not presented as a source of investment, tax, or legal advice. You should not rely on statements or representations made within the book or by any externally referenced sources. If you need investment, tax, or legal advice upon which you intend to rely in the course of your financial, business, or legal affairs, consult a competent, independent financial advisor, accountant, or attorney.

The contents of this book should not be taken as financial or legal advice, or as an offer to buy or sell any securities, fund, type of fund, or financial instruments. It should not be taken as an endorsement or recommendation of any particular company or individual, and no responsibility can be taken for inaccuracies, omissions, or errors. The information presented is not to be considered investment or legal advice. The reader should consult a Registered Investment Advisor or registered dealer or attorney prior to making any investment or legal decision.

The author does not assume any responsibility for actions or non-actions taken by people who have read this book, and no one shall be entitled to a claim for detrimental reliance based upon any information provided or expressed herein. Your use of any information provided herein does not constitute any type of contractual relationship between yourself and the provider(s) of this information. The author hereby disclaims all responsibility and liability for all use of any information provided in this book.

The materials here are not to be interpreted as establishing an attorney-client or any other relationship between the reader and the author or his firm.

Although great effort has been expended to ensure that only the most meaningful resources are referenced in these pages, the author does not endorse, guarantee, or warranty the accuracy, reliability, or thoroughness of any referenced information, product, or service. Any opinions, advice, statements, services, offers, or other information or content expressed or made available by third parties are those of the author(s) or publisher(s) alone. Reference to other sources of information does not constitute a referral, endorsement, or recommendation of any product or service. The existence of any particular reference is simply intended to imply potential interest to the reader.

The views expressed herein are exclusively those of the author and do not represent the views of any other person or any organization with which the author is, or may be, associated.

INDEX

Page numbers in **bold** indicate tables; those in *italics* indicate figures or photographs.

Stuart Veale is the president and founder of the Investment Performance Institute Inc., a firm that specializes in providing advanced-level practical capital markets training and consulting services to the financial services industry. Previously he was a senior vice president of portfolio strategy and design for the national sales group at Prudential Securities Inc. and senior vice president of advanced training at PaineWebber Inc.

Over the last 30 years, Mr. Veale has trained more than 6,000 capital markets professionals on portfolio design, trading strategies, risk analysis, derivative pricing and strategies, fixed income portfolio management, equity pricing and analysis, CFA I and II Prep, and numerous other securities-related topics. He has published six books: *The Handbook of the U.S. Capital Markets* (Harper Business), *Bond Yield Analysis* (New York Institute of Finance), *Tapping the Small Business Market* (New York Institute of Finance), *Essential Investment Math* (International Financial Press), *Essential Asset Allocation* (International Financial Press), and *Stocks, Bonds, Options, Futures* (Prentice Hall Press). He has also published numerous financial articles in magazines such as *Registered Representative*, *Cash Flow Magazine*, and *Medical Economics*.